THE
GRUMPY
ACCOUNTANT

One Fed-Up Tax Pro's Practical Plan to Fix
Canada's Senselessly Complicated Tax System

NEAL WINOKUR, CPA, CA

ISBN (Paperback): 978-1-7772264-0-4
ISBN (e-Book): 978-1-7772264-1-1
ISBN (Audio Book): 978-1-7772264-2-8

Edited by: Catherine Leek of **Green Onion Publishing**
Interior Design and Layout by: Beth Crane of **WeMakeBooks.ca**
Cover Design by: Eli Parker

Printed and bound in Canada

To contact the author, e-mail:
neal@grumpyaccountant.ca

For sales discounts for volume orders, please contact:
neal@grumpyaccountant.ca

To contact the author with your tax nightmare story or to learn more about how you can get involved in the movement for tax simplification, e-mail: neal@grumpyaccountant.ca and visit www.grumpyaccountant.ca.

To my dear wife Ali
Thank you for miraculously tolerating me and encouraging me to write down my thoughts instead of constantly complaining to you.

To my daughter Olivia
May you grow up in a Canada with a simple tax system.

And lastly, to every single Canadian suffering unnecessarily due to our ridiculous, antiquated, complicated tax system.

May we soon be freed from this insane tax filing nightmare.

THE MAKING OF A GRUMPY ACCOUNTANT

When I started working as a young, naïve accountant, I was eager, enthusiastic and excited for the career that lay ahead. I slogged through four years of drudgery to obtain my professional designation. I then spent the next seven years, at the time of this writing, running my own accounting practice.

I have filed countless tax returns throughout the course of my work. During this time, I have become increasingly frustrated as I came to understand how complicated and inefficient our tax system is.

I have seen how honest, hard-working people get ensnared in the maze of an uncompassionate and faceless bureaucracy. Canadians spend approximately $7 billion every year to file their individual income tax returns, averaging $501 per household.[1]

I have seen how maddening and convoluted it can be to deal with the Canada Revenue Agency (CRA), which has an annual budget of $4.3 billion[2] and growing. The CRA employs 40,000 people whereas the Internal Revenue Service of the United States employs 80,000 people even though the population of the United States is 10 times the size of Canada.[3]

Many other countries, such as Spain, Estonia, Finland, Norway and Iceland,[4] have very simple tax systems in which the majority of taxpayers are not required to file a tax return. Ninety per cent of taxpayers in England, 87% of taxpayers in Denmark and 74% of taxpayers in Sweden do not have to file tax returns.[5] In Estonia, it takes the average person five minutes to file their tax return.[6] New Zealand has become the master of tax reform.[7]

If all these countries have a straightforward tax system, why don't we?

My dream is for the tax system to be massively simplified, at least for the majority of taxpayers and especially for those on the lowest end and in the middle of the income spectrum. People should be able to file their own tax returns without the need to purchase software or hire grumpy accountants like me.

Imagine if we could make changes to our tax system that resulted in a revenue-neutral impact to the government, such that government spending could remain at the same levels they are at now. Imagine if the system of collecting individual income tax was streamlined to a point where millions of Canadians could save hundreds of dollars a year on accounting fees, as well as saving the time, stress and effort involved in filing their tax returns.

Canadians from across the entire political spectrum must rally and work together on this very important issue. Even if Canadians disagree on whether or not we are paying too little or too much tax, we must all agree that the system under which we are obligated to file our tax returns must be made less complex and more efficient.

I wrote this book, because every night I lie awake in bed, unable to fall asleep, thinking about how strange it is that I have a job as a tax accountant. I truly believe it is shameful that my job is necessary.

I can no longer stand idly by while millions of us continue to suffer under this stress-inducing and expensive tax-filing regime. I feel a moral obligation to publicly call on our politicians to massively simplify our tax system as soon as possible.

Until my dream of a straightforward tax system comes true, *The Grumpy Accountant* will share critical tips on how ordinary Canadians can survive the mess of our tax system. These are based on my experience of seeing the most common pitfalls and tax traps that people fall into.

This book is written in plain, easy-to-read language so every single Canadian can understand. We will see how Jerry, a fictional character symbolizing the average Canadian, experiences the inefficiency of the tax system as a student, an employee, a married man, a parent, an entrepreneur, a retiree and even as a dead guy as he is taxed beyond the grave. The tax traps, mistakes and nightmares that Jerry faces are based on real-life, true stories that my clients have experienced.

Jerry's grumpy accountant, George, will be there every step of the way to help him along and propose ideas on how to streamline the system once and for all.

CONTENTS

The Making of a Grumpy Accountant v

CHAPTER 1 — Why is My Pay Cheque So Low? 1

Jerry receives his first pay stub and is clueless.

He meets his accountant, George, who appears all knowing and wise as he explains everything clearly, but grumpily!

CHAPTER 2 — Are Tax Refunds a Huge Scam? 9

Jerry receives his first big juicy tax refund.

He's overjoyed until George ruins his parade as he explains how tax refunds are a bit of scam.

CHAPTER 3 — No, You Cannot Deduct the Cost of Your Clothes! 21

Jerry wonders why he can't claim the cost of his suits and commuting as deductions on his tax return.

CHAPTER 4 — The Wonderful World of CRA Audits 27

Jerry is audited by the Canada Revenue Agency!

He is worried, saddened and his soul is crushed.

George guides him along and offers some ideas on how to completely simplify the tax system such that CRA audits, and even the obligation to file a tax return, would be a thing of the past.

CHAPTER 5 — You Mean I Can Travel Back in Time? 39

Jerry can't believe he can adjust past year tax returns going back for ten years.

He is overjoyed as he receives another big juicy tax refund, although it costs him a lot of time and fees.

CHAPTER 6 — What's the Deal with GST Credits? 45

Jerry receives some pennies back from the government even though he's paying a lot of income tax. George proposes a guaranteed minimum income or a negative income tax to completely simplify Canada's overly complicated and inefficient system of welfare, credits and benefits.

CHAPTER 7 — Take the Bonus 53

Jerry starts making more money but has to pay higher rates of tax. He wonders if it's worth it.

CHAPTER 8 — Can the CRA Just Make Stuff Up? 59

Jerry's girlfriend, Elaine, has a roommate named Pam with an arbitrary assessment problem. Can George work his magic and save Pam?

CHAPTER 9 — Why Does the CRA Charge So Many Penalties? 67

Jerry can't believe how the richest Canadians get sweet deals from the CRA to waive penalties and interest but average people with low and modest incomes have a hard time fighting the penalties and interest they are charged.

George recommends some sensible ideas on how to fix the penalties and interest regime to be fairer.

CHAPTER 10 — Love and Marriage 75

Jerry and Elaine wonder why they can't file one tax return as a family.

CHAPTER 11 — Home Sweet Home 83

Jerry almost has a heart attack when he finds out he has to report the sale of a home on his tax return.

CHAPTER 12 — Children—Little Bundles of Tax Benefits 89

Jerry and Elaine are upset when they see how the government double dips.

A family's tax bill is calculated based on each individual spouse's income but the amount of Canada Child Benefits a family is entitled to receive is based on combined family income.

CHAPTER 13 — Kids are Expensive; Government is Here to Help, or Are They? 97

Elaine can't believe how complicated it is for her to become an employer and hire a nanny for her children.

CHAPTER 14 — How to Save Money 103

RRSPs, TFSAs, RESPs, RRIFs, and more.

Jerry and Elaine are overwhelmed with how the tax system makes saving money very complicated.

George clarifies everything while explaining some general tax consequences around investing.

CHAPTER 15 — The Hardship of Being a Self-Employed Tax Collector 115

Jerry can't believe he must now become a tax collector for the government as a reward for starting his own business.

George helps him along as Jerry registers for GST. George explains all the problems, pitfalls and insanity of the current GST system and suggests ideas on how to fix it in order to save self-employed people huge hassles.

CHAPTER 16 — One Equals Two—Double CPP 129

Jerry is shocked when he learns he must pay double the amount of CPP now that he is self-employed.

George, once again, presents some great advice and tips on how he can continue to survive and thrive as a self-employed individual under the Canadian tax regime.

CHAPTER 17 — Are Corporations Evil Legal Fictions? 137

Jerry incorporates his business and experiences even more ridiculous bureaucracy. George guides him along as usual.

CHAPTER 18 — It's Not You; It's Me 147

Jerry pays himself a salary from his business but can't believe the complexity involved. George provides the best advice and tells Jerry of the two-year bureaucratic nightmare another client faced.

CHAPTER 19 — Paying Tax on Imaginary Income 155

Jerry's business loses money but he still has to pay tax due to rules regarding capital assets, depreciation and accounts receivable. He is sad, confused and utterly frustrated. George advances more ideas on how to fix the tax system such that small-business owners and the self-employed would never again pay tax on income that doesn't exist in reality.

CHAPTER 20 — The Golden Years 165

Jerry and Elaine are approaching retirement. George helps them understand the extremely complicated, illogical and impossible-to-understand Canadian retirement system—GIS, OAS, CPP, RRSPs, TFSAs, RRIFs, pension income splitting and more.

George proposes more ideas on how to improve and simplify the system.

CHAPTER 21 — Death and Taxes—There is No Escape 179

Final tax return, deemed disposition at death, paying tax on unrealized gains, estate tax returns ... it never ends!

CHAPTER 22 — My Dream for the Future 187

George proffers his vision of what a very simple, friendly, easy, efficient
tax system could look like. He makes one final desperate plea for Canadians
to wake up and start a peaceful movement to make tax simplification an
important countrywide, non-partisan urgent issue.

Endnotes 197

Resources 201

Acknowledgements 207

Index 209

Chapter 1

WHY IS MY PAY CHEQUE SO LOW?

It was Monday morning, and, for Jerry, it was his first-ever Monday morning of his first day at his new job. He finally graduated from university where he studied architecture and was genuinely excited to begin the next phase of his life.

He arrived at work and his first order of business was to meet with the human resources department for an orientation. What in the world does it mean to be a "human resource" he thought to himself. Regardless, he had no time to ponder these great mysteries. He had forms to fill out.

He looked at the forms. They were strange and meaningless to him. There was one form for the federal government and another for the province. He had no idea how to fill them out. Each form had a list of "tax deductions" that he could fill out or leave blank. He had to fill in his social insurance number, which he didn't know off hand.

Jerry was flabbergasted. He had worked odd jobs throughout high school and university. Some of them were unpaid internships and others were informal. He didn't remember anything about filling out official-looking forms.

In all of his years in high school and university, he never learnt about any of these concepts. He felt lost and dejected. He was very embarrassed as he told the human resources employees that he must call his parents to ask them how he should fill out these forms. His parents told him his social insurance number but otherwise were unable to help him as they also had no idea what these forms were.

Please note: Numbers throughout the book have been rounded and simplified for easier readability.

1

The human resources employees giggled but were helpful and reassuring. They helped him to fill out the forms as best he could.

The next few days went by without a hiccup. He settled into his new job and felt very lucky to find a position in one of the top architectural firms in the country.

On Friday of his second week of work, his co-workers in the other cubicles were very excited. There was a feeling in the air that he never experienced before. It was pay day. Today he would receive his first pay cheque for his first two weeks of work. He was ready. He had worked hard for so long, throughout high school and university, and at his first two weeks of work. Finally, hard work was starting to pay off.

An envelope was placed on Jerry's desk. He eagerly opened it, full of excitement and anticipation. Based on his salary of $40,000, he was anticipating a cheque in the amount of $1,500 for his first two weeks of work.[8] He looked at the cheque and noticed something very strange. The cheque was for only $1,200.[9] It was missing $300.

He thought there must be some mistake. He then noticed another large piece of paper attached to the cheque that was entitled "pay stub."

Jerry examined the pay stub very closely. He noticed that there was one amount called "gross pay," and then there were several deductions such as "CPP," "EI," "federal income tax," "provincial income tax" and finally "net pay."

The gross pay was in fact $1,500 as he expected. But he had no idea what all these other strange letters and words meant. Why were these deductions so high? He was only earning $40,000 for the year and he felt he needed every penny, considering he still had student loans to pay off. Jerry vaguely remembered his parents frequently complaining of high taxes but he never imagined this would happen to him.

Jerry went home and prepared to go out to a friend's birthday party. At the party, Jerry regaled his friends with stories from his first two weeks of work. He explained what happened with the pay cheque and pay stub and suddenly became very sad and gloomy.

One of the young women there, who Jerry had never seen before, approached Jerry and introduced herself. "I have to tell you something. Back where I come from, across the pond in England, I never had to file a tax return. When I moved here to Canada, I thought it was so bizarre that almost everyone has to file a tax return. I felt completely lost so I asked around and I found a really good accountant. Perhaps you should meet with him and he can teach you everything you need to know."

Jerry was thankful for this advice. "Thanks, that sounds great. My name's Jerry by the way. And you are?"

"Elaine," she replied.

They shook hands and she provided Jerry with the contact information of her accountant. They continued talking and getting to know each other. Jerry was enamored by her British accent and all his sadness and gloominess disappeared for the rest of the night.

Jerry called the accountant first thing Monday morning. Jerry's first impression from the phone call was not that great. The accountant sounded exhausted and frustrated. Jerry was having second thoughts but decided to meet with him, so that he would have something interesting to talk about with Elaine.

Jerry walked into the accountant's office. He looked around and noticed that there were boxes of paper and files laying around everywhere. The ceiling had dreary fluorescent lights, which have been known to cause headaches. There were no windows. The walls looked like they were something out of a 1970s movie. It clearly had not been updated in a long time.

The accountant stood up from his chair to greet Jerry. Jerry looked at him carefully. The accountant appeared to be much younger than Jerry originally assumed he would be, perhaps only ten years older than himself. Despite his youthful looks, he seemed to be quite stressed out. He looked very tired and had large bags under his eyes. His hair was all over the place. His shirt was untucked, his facial hair was unkempt and overall he seemed to be a mess.

Jerry noticed a poster on the wall above the desk. It was a First World War poster depicting Canadian soldiers in the trenches. He thought this seemed quite out of place for an accountant.

The accountant introduced himself, "Hello, thanks for coming in. My name is George. It's nice to meet you. Why don't you have a seat? We have a lot to talk about."

Jerry sat down, showed him his pay stub and asked his new accountant if the pay stub was correct.

"Jerry, believe it or not, your pay stub is 100% accurate. Your employer is obligated to deduct all those amounts from your pay."

"Okay, but what are all these strange letters and acronyms? CPP? EI? I feel so lost; I don't understand any of this."

"Don't worry Jerry, I will explain everything. It's not as bad as it seems. It's bad, but not that bad. It could be worse. The first deduction is 'CPP.' This refers to the 'Canada Pension Plan.' These are payments that go towards a pension that will be paid out to you when you retire. 'EI' refers to 'Employment Insurance' and these funds are used to pay out benefits to workers who lose their jobs or go on sick leave, parental leave or for other similar situations. Lastly, the income taxes are sent to the federal and provincial governments to pay for all of the services and functions that we expect our governments to provide."

"Okay, so let me get this straight. CPP is my pension, EI goes into a fund that I can access benefits from if I become sick or lose my job and the rest is income tax?"

"You got it. The important thing will be your T4 slip. Your employer will give you a copy of your T4 slip after the end of the year and will file it with the Canada Revenue Agency—or CRA is the abbreviation that is often used. Once you have your T4, you need to send it to me so I can file your tax return."

"File my what?"

George sat back in his chair and smiled. "You need to file a tax return every year."

"But why? You just finished explaining that my employer is taking off all the taxes from each pay cheque and filing my T4 with the CRA so why do I need to file a tax return?"

George smiled again, "Jerry, let me show you something. You see this?"

George placed in Jerry's lap a 50-page document that looked freshly printed. Jerry glanced down at the 50 pages and stared back at George with a look of complete confusion on his face.

"Jerry, this is an example of a tax return I am about to file for a client. These 50 pages represent the client's copy of the tax return that I will send him for his records. I will then 'e-file' his tax return electronically. Welcome to the Canadian tax system. Your T4 is not your tax return. You might be able to get a tax refund because you are entitled to claim a huge list of tax deductions and tax credits. Don't worry. I will take care of everything for you. Now, we need to discuss my fees."

Jerry was overwhelmed; this was a lot of information to take in all at once. George could sense Jerry's stress level. He had dealt with these types of situations countless times before. He proceeded to calm Jerry down.

"Look, there's a lot more to say but don't worry. I will be here every step of the way. I am here for you, Jerry. And when I'm not here for you, I'm there for you! You should know you have other options you can use to file your tax return. You can download TurboTax or UFile or go to www.simpletax.ca and file your tax return by yourself using the CRA auto-fill system."

"George, you know what, I wouldn't even know where to begin if I tried filing my own tax return. Even though I would save a bit of money each year if I filed for myself, I feel like it would take me forever to figure out this stuff all alone. I will gladly pay your fee. Thanks so much for meeting with me today. I sort of—just sort of—feel a little better."

As Jerry was leaving the office, he took one last look at that First World War poster. George saw that Jerry was staring at the poster trying to understand what it was doing there.

"Jerry, believe it or not, I am not a war buff. That poster is there to remind me of the history of the income tax in Canada. From 1867 to 1917, there was no federal income tax. In 1917, the government was running out of money due to the expenses of the First World War, which was raging on at that time. They introduced the *Income War Measures Act* to help fund the war effort. The legislation was only 11 pages long, could be read in 20 minutes and only forced the top 2% of income earners to pay income tax and file a tax return.

"The income tax was supposed to be a temporary measure to pay off the debts from the war. Of course, we still have the income tax today, over 100 years later. Except, today the *Income Tax Act* is over 3,000 pages, contains over 1,000,000 words and forces almost every Canadian to file a tax return. Every day I look at the poster and it reminds me of my dream to simplify the tax system and reduce the *Income Tax Act* from 3,000 pages back to the original 11!"

Jerry was fascinated by this piece of history. He thanked George for his time and was very thankful that Elaine made the introduction. He knew he had to call Elaine and ask her for the opportunity to thank her in person over dinner. But he was so exhausted from the meeting, when he arrived home, he went straight to bed. He didn't sleep well that night but he did feel relieved a professional tax filer was going to be on his side.

TIP #1 — *Look at Your Pay Stubs*

I often wonder if people look at their pay stubs. It's very important to ensure your employer is not making mistakes when paying you. The deductions from your pay can be complicated so it's not unheard of for employers to make errors in their calculations.

Whether you are paid weekly, bi-weekly, semi-monthly or monthly, it's always a good idea to look at your pay stub in order to ensure its accuracy. There are tools online that can help you verify these amounts. I have included links to these tools in the Resources at the back of this book.

I also recommend you keep copies of all your pay stubs just in case there is a problem with your T4. The amounts showing on your T4 slip should agree with the year-to-date amounts on the last pay stub you received for the year, in theory.

If you look at your pay stub right now and feel lost, don't worry; by the end of this book, you'll be a master. Or, at the very least, have a better understanding than you do now.

Chapter 2

Are Tax Refunds a Huge Scam?

Elaine agreed to meet Jerry for dinner. He told her how helpful George was and thanked her profusely for introducing them. Jerry learnt a lot about Elaine that night. Turns out she was an editor at a respected magazine. She enjoyed her work immensely despite the stress of constant deadlines. She told Jerry about her life back in England; she missed her family back home but was enjoying living in Canada, despite the more complicated tax system. They had a nice evening and agreed to continue to stay in touch.

Jerry continued going to work day in and day out. As time went on, he was getting a bit restless, even a little bored. But he was thankful to have a job that paid the bills.

One day, during the dreary cold snowy month of February he went to retrieve his mail. He noticed a mysterious envelope from his employer. He had no idea what this could be. He held the envelope in his hands, looking at it, and although he was not a religious man, he fervently prayed that he was not going to be summoned to the human resources department or even worse. He opened the envelope and he grabbed the piece of paper inside, unfolded it and there it was, in all its glory—a T4 slip.

Jerry recalled that George had mentioned he would receive a T4 slip. Jerry knew he had to call him and inform him of this monumental event. George asked Jerry to bring the slip with him to his office.

Jerry brought in the T4 slip and George began preparing his tax return. George asked Jerry many strange, and somewhat boring, questions such

Please note: Numbers throughout the book have been rounded and simplified for easier readability.

as "Are you married or living common law? Do you own foreign property that cost $100,000 or more? Do you have any children or other dependants? Do you have any disabilities? Are you a volunteer firefighter? Did you pay interest on student loans? Do you live in northern Ontario? Did you pay for any medical expenses? Did you make any donations last year? Did you make any RRSP contributions—sorry, any contributions to a Registered Retirement Savings Plan? Did you make any contributions to any political parties? Did you move more than 40 kilometres to start a new job?"

Jerry laughed at some of these questions and could not believe why all this information was necessary to file his tax return. He did not understand what was going on. He felt unprepared and was worried he would be missing important information.

He told George he did, in fact, have medical expenses that were not covered by insurance or the government, he was still paying off his student loans and he made a few donations as well. Jerry had no idea that all of this would affect his taxes, but he was able to access the information.

George inputted all the information into his trusted tax software and, lo and behold, George informed Jerry of some good news. "Jerry, you will be receiving a tax refund of $2,000."

Jerry was very excited. He could not believe his ears. He had heard of people receiving tax refunds before. He remembered reading in the news every year, around March and April, all the articles about what to do with your tax refund. Some people suggested investing it in a TFSA, whatever that was, or paying down debt or spending it on a new TV.

Jerry said, "Wow, what an amazing government and amazing tax system we have in Canada."

Jerry thanked George and was now truly amazed with his accountant. He thought that he had the best accountant in the country, maybe even the world. He told George that he would refer him to all his family and friends.

George the accountant responded, "Jerry, I know you think I am a genius and I know you are very happy to receive your tax refund.

Unfortunately, I must tell you the sad truth of what this tax refund means. Please know that what I am telling you might shock you but it is true, every word of it."

Jerry was nervous but he hunkered down and listened intently.

George continued, "Everyone loves receiving their tax refund. However, many people do not realize that a 'tax refund' is really just an interest-free loan to the government."

"George, what do you mean a loan to the government? I didn't loan the government money. I think I would know if I loaned the government money."

"But, Jerry, you did loan the government money. And you didn't even charge them interest. I hope you never start a bank because if you don't charge interest on loans, you probably won't make much money. The government took too much tax from you during the year; they did not pay any interest to you for your money while they had it all year; and now look how happy you are to receive this money back.

"This system—of tax refunds—is a great sleight of hand by the government. Think about it. The majority of tax filers in Canada are like you, Jerry. They are employees. In fact, for the 2018 tax year, over 18 million Canadians received tax refunds, totaling over $32 billion."[10]

"Wow, $32 billion! That's a significant amount of money. So, you mean, the government collected an extra $32 billion in income tax throughout the year, and then had to refund it back to taxpayers."

"Exactly. Many of these people think that the government is benevolent and generous. Some of these people think they are actually making money and that the government is so amazing because it's giving them free money. What these people fail to realize is that this was their money in the first place. The government is not being benevolent or generous. In fact, it is quite the opposite.

"The government knows that it cannot expect these 18 million Canadians to actually physically pay the government thousands of dollars of tax at the end of each year. So instead, the government forces employers to deduct income tax directly from their employees' pay.

"Jerry, remember when you first came to me and showed me your pay stub? The taxes were deducted from each pay cheque but how were those amounts calculated? That calculation did not take into account the fact that you had medical expenses, student loan interest and donations to claim. So how is that fair?

"The amount of tax that was deducted from each of your pay cheques should have been $2,000 less for the year which amounts to $167 each month. Imagine, Jerry, if your net pay each month was $167 higher. Wouldn't you rather have that money throughout the year so you can have better cash flow? You could have used that money to pay down your student loans faster, invest and earn investment income, or take Elaine to nicer restaurants."

"George, how do you know about Elaine and I?"

"Jerry, I'm an accountant. My clients, including Elaine, tell me everything. Anyways, I believe that the current system is set up to keep the majority of people happy and complacent. The majority of taxpayers have their taxes deducted throughout the year without them lifting a finger, so these people do not actually feel the pain of physically paying taxes to the government.

"You felt so good when I told you about your tax refund. You are now going to look forward to filing a tax return every year in anticipation of this refund. It is quite an amazing feat the government achieved, fooling the majority of tax paying citizens into enjoying and looking forward to tax time so they can receive a refund.

"The 'tax refund' should be renamed to 'government took too much of your money throughout the year and is now returning it to you without paying you interest.'"

Jerry was quiet for a few moments trying to take in all this information. Jerry then thought of something. "George, that is wild. My head is spinning.

I have only one question. I would like the increased cash flow throughout the year, as you described. Is there a way I can have less tax taken off my pay cheques throughout the year instead of waiting for my refund at the end of the year?"

George smiled, "Oh Jerry, if only it were that simple. When you first started working, you should have filled out a TD1 form. Do you remember filling that out?"

"Yes, I do. The human resources department had to walk me through it."

"That form allows your employer to deduct less tax from your pay if you claim any of the 'standard' tax credits on your tax return, such as the Disability Tax Credit or spousal amount or a few others. But that form does not include the credits that you claimed—medical expenses, student loan interest and donations and anything else we can claim. For these types of deductions your human resources department cannot agree to withhold less tax unless a form is filed with the CRA. This is Form T1213 'Request to Reduce Tax Deductions at Source.' Once you file this form and it is approved by the CRA, your employer can deduct less tax, which will increase your cash flow throughout the year."

Jerry thought for a moment. "Wait a minute, you mean if I want to keep more of my own money during the year, I actually have to fill out a form and request that the government let me keep my own money and it is subject to their approval?"

"Yes, exactly! Welcome to Canada's income tax system. Oh, and by the way, this form must be filed and approved every year in order to have the same effect every year."

Jerry had a shocked look on his face.

George continued, "I think you're starting to see the insanity of our tax system. In order to keep your money that you work hard for, you must request permission from the government before the start of that year.

"The vast majority of people do not know about this form. Jerry, you are one of the lucky few who are even aware of this. If a taxpayer wants the correct amount of tax to be deducted based on their actual deductions and credits, then the burden is on them—you—the taxpayer—to file a form with the CRA to make the request and the CRA must approve the request."

Jerry interrupted, "Why is the system like this? I don't understand. Why don't I just pay the correct amount of tax at the end of the year and the employer not deduct anything?"

George laughed at this suggestion. "The defenders of the current system claim that this is the most efficient way for the government to collect income taxes from every individual. They worry that if employers were not forced to deduct the income tax from their employees' pay, then the employees would not save their income throughout the year to pay their tax. Sadly, they are probably right.

"But I believe that they are actually worried that there would be a massive tax revolt when all these people realize how much tax they are actually paying—if they had to physically make the payments themselves at the end of every year."

"George, is there any way to fix this? I mean, after all, the government needs to collect tax from people."

George relished when his clients asked him these types of questions. He smiled and said, "We can definitely find ways to make the tax system a lot simpler. For example, we could eliminate all tax deductions and all tax credits and then simply lower the tax rate to make up for it. That's it. It's so simple, so easy and so logical. Most taxpayers, employees like you, would not even have to file a tax return. The T4 slip that your employer sends to CRA on your behalf would become your tax return. The tax deducted from your pay would be the correct and final amount and then you would not have to file a tax return."

"I don't understand. What about the medical expenses? What about the student loan interest, and the donations? How can you propose to abolish all these deductions and credits? According to your plan, I would not receive my juicy tax refund. Is that what you are saying?"

"True, you would not receive your juicy tax refund but remember the other half of my proposal—to lower the actual income tax rate. You wouldn't need any deductions or credits because there would be a lower tax rate in the first place. So everything would end up nice and even."

"George, this seems a bit far-fetched. Let me get this straight. You want to eliminate every single tax deduction and credit and then lower the actual tax rates?"

"Yes, exactly!"

George continued. "There are quite a few countries with a similar system in place already. Canada just needs to study how these countries operate their tax systems and follow their best practices.

"Currently, these deductions and credits that people love claiming reduce our tax bills by $130 billion per year.[11] Over the past 50 years, governments have added more and more deductions and credits into the tax system. They do this in order to target certain groups of voters and to encourage or discourage certain behaviours. It is quite patronizing that our politicians feel they must micro-manage the lives of Canadians by assigning a tax credit or a tax deduction to every life event (child care, medical expenses, disability, retirement savings, volunteer firefighter, caregiver, first-time home buyer, moving expenses, etc.).

"So if we transition to a simple tax system without any deductions and credits, all we need to do is lower the tax rates, starting at the lowest tax bracket, to ensure a revenue neutral result to the government."

"George, I am enthralled by this idea. But what do you mean by starting at the lowest bracket?"

"Good question. Currently, every Canadian is entitled to earn $13,229 of income without paying income tax on that amount.[12] The problem is that this amount is way too low. The low-income cut off, for an individual, is estimated to be between $13,000 and $21,000,[13] so why in the world are we charging income tax to people as soon as they hit an income of $13,229?

"If we eliminate tax on the lowest tax bracket, which would be the first $50,000[14] of income, this would mean that the lowest 65% of income earners would pay zero income tax[15] and Canadians would pay approximately $80 billion less in tax overall.[16]

"The next tax bracket, which applies to incomes between $50,000 and $97,000,[17] is taxed at 20.5% on the federal level. We can reduce this tax rate to 10% to save another $50 billion in taxes.[18]

"Thus, we have a revenue neutral plan to simplify the tax system. We get $80 billion by eliminating tax on income up to $50,000 and $50 billion by reducing the next tax bracket to a rate of 10%. This adds up to $130 billion.

"This would make the tax filing system incredibly easier. There would be no need to file a tax return. The only exception would be for people who are self-employed or those who earn investment income such as capital gains. But for the majority of taxpayers, who are employees, the T4, which is already filed by your employer, would be your tax return. There would no need for tax refunds, no need for hiring grumpy, expensive accountants like me to file your tax return and no need for dealing with a complicated bureaucracy anymore."

"George, do you think this will ever happen? Can this idea ever become a reality in Canada?"

"Well, it would be my dream come true. But even under the current system, someone who is receiving a huge refund every year should have the choice of having less tax deducted from each cheque without any requirements to file any forms or seek approval from the CRA.

"You should be able to go to your payroll department, show them your tax return from the prior year that shows a big juicy refund. They would deduct the right amount of tax based on amounts from your prior year's tax return. This will save time and money as well for the CRA since it will be one less useless bureaucratic form to process."

Jerry thought this sounded reasonable but wondered if the government would ever listen to or implement this idea. He was no longer happy to receive his big juicy $2,000 refund because he realized this money would have helped him throughout the year if it was added to every pay cheque. He decided to file the required form to allow his employer to deduct less pay from each cheque as George suggested.

George warned him that if he didn't have the same credits and deductions then he might owe tax at the end of the year but Jerry insisted he would have the same credits and deductions as the year before.

A couple weeks later Jerry received a brown envelope in the mail and the labeling indicated it was from the Canada Revenue Agency. Jerry could not contain his excitement. He opened the envelope and there was a strange letter called a "Notice of Assessment." Jerry had no idea what that meant. He tried to read it but it all looked like complete gibberish to him. He did, however, notice there was a cheque for $2,000. He jumped up and down with joy; he immediately deposited his tax refund cheque into his bank account to save for future use.

He began planning another dinner with Elaine. He wanted to tell her all about his tax refund. He thought that would really excite her. Jerry went to sleep that night in a great mood and felt perfectly at ease with the world.

TIP #2 — *Set Up "My Account" with CRA Online*

You will receive your T4 slip from your employer before the end of February for the previous year. Whoever files your tax return will need this important document.

If you misplace your T4, you can obtain your T4 slip, along with other important tax information online if you set up "My Account" on the CRA website. The link can be found in the Resources at the end of this book. This is a great tool where you can access your past ten years of tax returns, Notices of Assessments, your RRSP and TFSA contribution room, other carry-forward amounts, many other T slips and other such information.

I highly recommend setting this up as it will help you avoid the need to call the CRA in many situations saving you significant time. For example, if you need to update your address with CRA, this can now be done online through "My Account."

Also, if you are trying to file your own tax return with CRA-certified software, you will be able to use the "auto-fill" function in that software to automatically download your T4 slip and other tax information CRA already has on file. Check the Resources section at the back of the book for links to various do-it-yourself tax software.

TIP #3 — *Lower Your Tax Deductions from Your Pay*

If you currently receive a large tax refund every year, and you would rather keep that money throughout the year instead of waiting until tax refund time, then fill out and file Form T1213 "Request to Reduce Tax Deductions at Source." This form can be found on the CRA website and the link to the form is listed in the Resources at the back of this book.

Some people prefer receiving their tax refund once a year, in one shot, because they aren't exactly sure if they will have the same credits or deductions every year. So this comes down to personal preference and your specific situation.

If you know you have the exact same credits and deductions each year and your refund amount is consistent annually, then you might want to consider filing this form. But if your refund fluctuates year to year, then this might not be for you.

TIP # 4 — *How to File Your Tax Return*

There are so many different ways you can file your tax return these days.

1. **"File My Return:"** This is an automated phone service directly from the CRA for eligible individuals with low or fixed income. If you are eligible for this service, the CRA will send you a letter.

2. **Mail:** You can mail your tax return to the CRA the old-fashioned way. Print the tax return, include copies of your T slips and other receipts and mail the tax return to your Tax Centre.

3. **Netfile:** In order to "netfile" your tax return, you must purchase CRA-Netfile-Certified software, of which there are many, and prepare your tax return using the software's instructions and guides. Be sure to save a copy of the tax return to a PDF file to keep it for your own files. Keep copies of all your receipts and documents in case CRA asks to see any documentation.

4. **E-File:** This is the method accountants and other professional tax filers use to electronically file tax returns on behalf of their clients.

5. **Free Tax Clinics:** People with modest incomes and simple tax situations are usually eligible to go to a free tax clinic where volunteers will help file their tax return. You can find information about free tax clinics on the CRA website.

Chapter 3

No, You Cannot Deduct the Cost of Your Clothes!

The next day, while Jerry was sitting on the bus on his way to work, a thought popped into his head. He realized that he was spending quite a lot of money, almost $1,800 per year, to take the bus to and from work every day. He wondered why he was not allowed to claim this as an expense on his tax return. After all, if he didn't spend this money, he wouldn't be able to arrive at work.

He thought of all the people who drive to and from work and he recognized that must get pretty expensive. Why would these people not be able to claim the cost related to driving to and from work?

He then looked down at the fancy expensive suit he was wearing. He considered that had he not been working, there was no way he would ever buy a suit like this. The price of the suit was paid out in order for him to go to work. It was a direct cost of being employed. He was obligated to wear business appropriate attire and yet he was pretty sure he was not allowed to claim this as an expense on his tax return.

When he arrived at work, he called George to discuss these ideas. He thought it seemed very logical that he should be able to claim these expenses, so he wanted to make sure that nothing was left out of his tax return.

"George, I know you filed my tax return already. I apologize for bringing this up now. But why can't I claim the cost of the suits and other clothing that are specifically purchased in order to wear at work? Why can't I claim the cost of the public transit expenses I must purchase in order to arrive at work every day? These are expenses I incur expressly because of the fact that I am working so are you sure you didn't miss these amounts on my tax return?"

"Jerry, you are a wise young man. You are speaking very logically, but sadly, our tax system is not logical. There used to be a tax credit available for people to claim their public transit passes but, alas, that tax credit no longer exists.[19] Clothing is not permitted to be claimed on your tax return and neither are the costs of driving to and from work. But you raise a very good question."

"Thanks, George. So I'm not crazy after all?"

"No, I don't think you are crazy. Think about it. If you weren't working, would you buy that suit? If you weren't working, would you pay for that public transit monthly pass?

"Or think about it this way, if you refused to buy suits or business appropriate attire and showed up at your job interview in a pair of jeans and a t-shirt, do you think you would actually get the job?

"And most jobs require you to be there in person on a daily basis. So why can't one claim the costs of commuting to and from work?

"Most jobs require you to wear clothing. Can you imagine if you showed up at work completely naked? It's true, there is good naked and there is bad naked, but showing up at work completely naked is definitely bad naked. I don't know anyone that would recommend trying that. Clothing is absolutely required in the workplace, so why wouldn't business clothing be a valid deduction?

"Jerry, the idea that the income tax rate should be based on your net income is a very important one."

"What do you mean by net income?"

"Net income refers to your income after taking into account expenses that you paid in order to earn that income. Imagine if you were self-employed and had your own business. You would be able to deduct all valid business expenses that you paid for in order to earn your income.

"Your taxes are calculated as: gross income minus expenses equals net income. Then, tax is calculated on the net income. So if self-employed people and business owners can claim expenses, why can't employees? After all, you have expenses too."

"So are you saying people like me, employees, simply cannot claim any expenses at all?"

"Unfortunately, our tax system only allows employees to claim expenses in very limited circumstances. They must have a form—Form T2200 'Declaration of Conditions of Employment'—filled out and signed by their employer. This form details the type of expenses they were obligated to incur as a result of their employment. For example, if someone works from home more than 50% of the time, they can claim some costs related to maintaining their home office. Or if someone must drive to different locations, other than their regular place of work, then they may be able to claim car expenses."

"So, George, can I claim some expenses, like my commuting expenses as per that Form T2200 you mentioned?"

"No, Jerry. That's only for people who drive around to many different locations. Driving to and from work, at the same location, does not count, so you are out of luck. Sorry to be the bearer of bad news."

"That's okay, George. So, in your opinion, do you think that employees like me should be able to claim their commuting and clothing expenses?"

"Well, in theory, yes, I do. They are a direct cost of your employment."

"But doesn't that contradict what you said before about your idea to eliminate all tax credits and deductions?"

"Yes, good point, Jerry. I don't think we should add more deductions into the tax system. Can you imagine the administrative nightmare? The CRA would have to do random audits on every employee in Canada, millions of people, claiming their car and clothing expenses. This would be so intrusive, so bothersome, so inefficient and so costly. People would have to keep all their receipts for every single gas fill-up and piece of clothing purchased. No thanks!

"Instead, the tax rates on employment income should be lowered to reflect the fact that people spend a lot of money to actually get to and from their jobs and spend money on clothing and other expenses that they can't claim, such as if they work from home less than 50% of the time. As I said before,[20] let's simply eliminate income tax on the first $50,000 of income and that would be fair to every single taxpayer and much simpler."

"George, you are a genius. Thanks for explaining all this. I hope you don't send me a bill for this extra conversation."

George rolled his eyes and hung up the phone.

TIP # 5 — *Employees Can Claim Some Expenses, Sometimes*

If you are an employee but are required to drive to many different locations as a part of your job, or if you work from home more than 50% of the time, you may be able to claim some expenses on your tax return. In order to claim these expenses, your employer must provide you with a filled out and signed Form T2200 "Declaration of Conditions of Employment." Then, when you file your tax return, you will need to claim these expenses on Form T777 "Statement of Employment Expenses." I have included a link to these forms in the Resources section at the back of the book.

Be careful with this, it can get complicated. And you will, of course, need to keep every single receipt for every single expense you want to claim in case the CRA audits your claim.

In addition, for car expenses, you will need to keep a log that tracks the number of kilometres you drive and details the trips you made that were for business purposes.

I have included some helpful expense tracking tools in the Resources section as well.

Chapter 4

THE WONDERFUL WORLD OF CRA AUDITS

M onths passed, the summer came and went. Jerry continued to work hard each and every day. He had spent a lot of time with Elaine over the summer. They began to date each other exclusively.

Jerry used his $2,000 tax refund to make additional payments towards his student loans as well as on some memorable dates with Elaine. He was enjoying life and felt like he was in a good place.

But then, everything changed. It was a crisp fall evening. Jerry was walking home from the bus stop after an uneventful day at work. He was admiring the beautiful fall colours, daydreaming of Elaine, when he went to obtain his mail. There was another brown envelope from the CRA. Jerry was nervous and confused. "What could this be?" he thought. He really had no idea what to expect.

He slowly and carefully opened the letter and was absolutely shocked at what he saw. The letter said "Notice of Reassessment" and had a whole bunch of numbers and gibberish that he did not understand. At the bottom of the reassessment, it said in big, huge, frightening, bold letters "BALANCE OWING: $1,000. PLEASE PAY WITHIN 14 DAYS TO AVOID ADDITIONAL INTEREST CHARGES."

Jerry almost fainted right then and there. He could not understand this at all. Why did he owe $1,000? He filed his tax return months ago and the CRA issued his tax refund of $2,000. He was very sad and scared. Where in the world would he find $1,000 and why did he even owe this money at all?

He could not make any sense of this so he called George and told him about the letter. George looked up Jerry's account on the CRA's "Represent a Client" system online. George did some digging and figured out exactly what happened.

He called Jerry back and told him, "Back in July, the CRA sent you a letter requesting to see your receipts for all your donations and medical expenses. It appears that you never received that letter, is that correct? Anyways, it does not matter now.

"The CRA says you never sent in the information they requested so they disallowed all the donations and medical expenses you claimed. They recalculated your tax return, without the donations and medical expenses, and now you have to pay them back $1,000. We can fix this by sending them copies of all the donation and medical receipts that they requested."

Jerry was very confused because he never received the letter from CRA in the first place. Jerry immediately gathered all the receipts and sent them to George. George submitted all the receipts to the CRA.

A month later, Jerry received a phone call from the CRA collections department asking him when he would pay the $1,000 balance owing. Jerry was very scared and did not know what to do so he called George.

George confirmed the call from CRA collections was not a scam; it was in fact the collections department. George told the collections department to hold off as the required information was sent in to be processed and once it was processed, the balance owing would be zero. The collections department understood and put the collections on hold for 90 days.

A few months later, Jerry received yet another brown envelope from the CRA. Once again, he nervously opened the envelope. There was another Notice of Reassessment that showed a balance owing of zero and an explanation that the CRA allowed the donation and medical expenses claimed as originally filed. Obviously, Jerry was very relieved and thanked George for his many efforts to fix this problem.

Jerry then said to his beloved accountant, "George, I don't understand something. How is it fair that the CRA can give out tax refunds to people and then many months later ask for the money back? Most people spend their tax refunds paying off debt or buying something or saving it for their future. If I had misplaced those donation and medical receipts and was unable to prove those amounts, where would I possibly come up with $1,000?"

"Jerry, that is a fine question. This is a great example of the problem with our tax system. The CRA reassesses tax returns after they have been filed and after the refunds have been paid out. The CRA can go back in time up to three years in the past, from the date of the assessment, to reassess tax returns. Technically, you actually have to keep all your receipts for all amounts claimed for six years! If the CRA suspects any fraud or wrongdoing, they can go back as many years as they feel necessary.

"What happened to you Jerry happens all the time to many taxpayers. The CRA issues a refund, benefit or credit to a taxpayer, and then many months or even years later demands that it be paid back.

"It cannot reasonably be expected that the taxpayer will keep their tax refunds on hand for six years in anticipation of a possible future reassessment.

"To put it simply, the vast majority of Canadians do not budget for unexpected tax bills but our tax system is designed in a way that often requires people to pay such surprises.

"The CRA issues tax refunds automatically within ten days to three weeks after someone files their tax return. Jerry, you received your refund pretty quickly. Most people do. The CRA does not bother to check for the accuracy of the tax returns before sending out the refunds. There are some tax returns where they do request backup documentation before issuing the refund. This is known as 'Pre-Assessment Review.'

"But most of the time, like what happened to you, they do a Post-Assessment Review, whereby they issue your refund first. Then a few months later, the CRA will send out a letter requesting backup documentation to verify some of the deductions and credits that you claimed. The problem is sometimes the taxpayers do not receive these letters.

"It really is an unfair and illogical system and causes taxpayers a lot of financial stress and pressure, especially for those with lower incomes and for those living pay cheque to pay cheque.

"In fact, there was a story reported by *Global News* that the CRA froze a Mississauga man's bank account and took out all the money from his work payroll even after they agreed to give him more time to pay his balance. Now the man is penniless and has no access to any money.[21]

"Another story described how a 94-year-old woman from Bradford, Ontario, had been harassed by the CRA with written demands for money even after a CRA agent said she owed nothing on her account.[22] The CRA claimed she owed them $1,200. The woman said, 'It's like a slap in the face.' A CRA agent on the phone said the written letters demanding payment would be discontinued but she kept receiving them and has been working to resolve the issue for more than a year.

"I have had many clients receive Notice of Assessments showing large balances of tax owing even though the taxpayers already paid off the balances. When I log into their accounts online, the account balance is zero and the payment they made shows up on their tax account. But when the CRA sends out the Notice of Assessments, for some unknown reason, they don't apply the payment onto the assessment, so the assessment shows a large balance owing. It's very distressing to taxpayers who have already paid their tax bill to receive an assessment weeks later showing the balance as still outstanding."

Jerry interjected, "Wow, I really would have had a hard time coming up with $1,000. I don't know what I would have done. Just thinking about it, I feel my blood pressure rising. I can't believe the CRA will freeze people's bank accounts and garnish their salaries to ensure their unexpected tax bills are paid off. Maybe your idea of eliminating all tax credits and deductions isn't so bad after all."

George smiled, "Yes, exactly. By abolishing all tax credits and deductions, we would solve this problem of CRA audits and unexpected tax bills. Your tax return would be the T4 slip that your employer already filed with the CRA. This way, there would never be a need for the CRA to send a letter to taxpayers requesting further documentation, no need for reassessments that go on for years and no need to keep receipts and documents for six years.

"I have seen cases where the CRA audits the same credits and deductions for the same taxpayers year after year. In some cases, were the claim to be disallowed, the additional tax payable would be minimal. It doesn't make any sense to conduct the audit in the first place.

"This system is very costly. Jerry, do you know why it costs $4.3 billion annually to fund the CRA? It's because of all these deductions and credits. The CRA spends $1 billion on 'Reporting Compliance,' $495 million on 'Collections and Returns Compliance,' $181 million on 'Appeals,' $2 million on 'Taxpayers' Ombudsman,' and $917 million on 'Internal Services.'[23] It's estimated that 74% of the total budget for the CRA is spent on personnel expenses such as salaries, allowances and benefits.[24] The other 26% of spending goes to accommodation and information technology related expenses."[25]

Jerry was silent in disbelief.

George continued, "Now even if we don't adopt my proposal, there should be a general rule for the CRA and all other government departments such as Service Canada to remedy this inefficient system.

"I wish the CRA or any other government department would never issue a tax refund, benefit or credit, whether it is a GST Credit, Canada Child Benefit, Old Age Security, or anything else, unless it is absolutely certain that the amount is correct and will have a zero per cent chance of future reassessment.

"If the CRA wants to examine your donation receipts or medical expenses, then they should do this verification first and only pay out the tax refund later. That is, in fact, how tax filing was done in the old days, before the internet, when people mailed paper copies of their tax returns to the CRA. They would also mail in all the receipts to prove the claims in their tax return.

"I have seen, on many occasions, the CRA sending out letters requesting repayment of GST Credits or Canada Child Benefits that were already paid out. Remember that it is generally people with lower incomes receiving these benefits so it's quite outrageous to expect these people to pay these amounts back.

"We need a system that respects taxpayers and respects the fact that many Canadians are in debt, living pay cheque to pay cheque and cannot afford to budget for unexpected tax bills."

Jerry was still confused about the Notice of Reassessment. "George, I don't understand why the CRA was so quick to claim that I owed them $1,000. I never received their letter, why didn't they call me or try to send another letter? Why didn't they give me more time to respond to them?"

"That's a good question. Sometimes they don't call people because people hang up on them for fear the call is fraudulent, from scammers pretending to be from the CRA. They usually send a letter on CRA letterhead and for the type of request they were making to see your receipts— they usually give you 30 days."

"Well, 30 days seems like enough time, I guess."

"Yes, it is understandable but actually a bit unfair considering how long the CRA takes to do everything on their end. Remember they wanted your receipts within 30 days but they took several months to reassess your tax return and remove the $1,000 balance owing on your account.

"Due to the behemoth tax system that we have allowed to form over the years, the CRA has a tremendous workload that is impossible to contend with. It is a ridiculous amount of inefficiency and bureaucracy. I'm sure you will see this in action, as many Canadians eventually do.

"Did you know the CRA receives more than 53 million calls per year? 53 million! If that's not bad enough, it's estimated that the CRA phone agents are giving wrong information 13% of the time to personal tax filers.[26]

"By the way, I don't blame the CRA. I blame every single Prime Minister and Minister of Finance over the past 50 years! A comprehensive review of the tax system has not taken place since The Carter Commission Report was released in 1967, so every government since that time is to blame for this mess. It is they who are responsible for making the necessary legislative changes to the tax system. Jerry, if you want real change, you need to contact your Member of Parliament, the Minister of Finance and the Prime Minister of Canada!"

"1967? That year sounds very familiar and iconic."

"That's because it's the last time the Toronto Maple Leafs won the Stanley Cup. I sometimes wonder what will come first—the Leafs winning the Cup or a comprehensive review and simplification of our tax system."

Jerry laughed. "George, only one of those is remotely realistic. Anyway, thanks again for everything. You're the best. I don't know what I would do without you."

Jerry left George's office with mixed feelings. He returned home to prepare for a relaxing evening with Elaine. He went over to her apartment where she served him a nice meal consisting of mutton, a big salad and coffee cake for dessert.

As they were eating, Elaine noticed Jerry was blankly staring at his plate. He wasn't talking much and seemed to be very distracted. "Jerry, what's the problem? You can tell me anything."

"Oh, Elaine, I don't want to bore you. But I had another meeting with George today and I can't stop thinking about how stressful all this tax stuff is. I've spent so much time, effort and accounting fees on dealing with these tax issues. I feel like George is getting rich off of me but I have no choice. I would be lost without him. I'm totally overwhelmed by it all."

Elaine smiled and reached across the table and held Jerry's hand. "Jerry, don't worry about that now. Just be relieved you have George by your side. He will take really good care of you."

TIP #6 — *Keep Every Receipt*

I cannot stress this enough. If you are going to claim a tax deduction or tax credit, you must—*absolutely must*—keep a copy of the receipt to prove the claim. You must keep this receipt for six years. I recommend keeping them even longer just in case. I also recommend keeping copies of your tax returns and notices of assessment for six previous tax years as well.

The CRA frequently audits the claims people make for Donation Tax Credits, medical expenses, child care deductions, first-time Home Buyers' Tax Credit and the list goes on and on. You are allowed to keep scanned copies of receipts as long as they are legible.

When you receive a letter from the CRA requesting to see documentation, it will definitely help the situation if you are already organized and able to provide everything in a timely manner.

If you need an extension, you can call the number on the letter and request another 30 days to gather the information.

If you are working with an accountant or tax preparer, you want to make his or her job as easy as possible. So have your receipts already organized.

Keep in mind that even if you use an accountant, tax preparer, H&R Block or any other such tax filing service, it is up to you to ensure your information in your tax return is complete and accurate.

I recommend everyone invest in a scanner or download one of the many scanning apps on their phone. Whenever you have a tax receipt that comes in throughout the year, simply scan it and either e-mail it directly to your tax preparer throughout the year or download it onto your own computer and have a folder of tax documents ready to go for tax filing time.

TIP #7 — *Beware of Scams*

There have been many scams over the years perpetrated by people within Canada and from overseas. They pretend to be from the CRA and demand you make a large payment immediately or you will be sent to prison. They even claim that the police are on their way to arrest you! Many Canadians, unfortunately, have fallen for these scams, and sent thousands of dollars to these cowardly people.

Here is how you can tell if someone contacting you is genuinely from the CRA or is in fact a scammer.

First, the CRA never sends e-transfers. If you receive an e-mail that claims to be an e-transfer from the CRA, it's a scam. Delete the e-mail right away. It should be noted that the CRA will directly deposit tax refunds, GST credits, Canada Child Benefits, etc., into your bank account, but only after you enroll for this service.

Second, the CRA does not send e-mails. If you receive an e-mail and it says it's from the CRA, delete it. If you signed up for "online mail," which you can do through your "My Account," then the CRA will send you an e-mail to tell you that you have online mail, but then you need to login to your CRA account to access the actual mail.

Third, if you receive a phone call from someone claiming to be a CRA agent and they say that you owe a sum of money and if you don't pay right away, there will be a judgment against you and the police are coming to get you, then hang up right away. Or instead of hanging up, keep them on the phone as long as possible, pretending to play dumb so that they have less time to scam other people. Ask them why they haven't mailed you a Notice of Reassessment or ask them for a statement of account on CRA letterhead if they claim you have a balance owing. You can check your CRA account online to see if there is, in fact, a balance owing. You can also hang up on them, and then call the actual CRA to determine your account balance.

I have included some common CRA phone numbers in the Resources section at the back of this book.

Be sure to report the fraudulent activity to the relevant authorities. See the Resources for how to report these fraudulent scams.

Chapter 5

You Mean I Can Travel Back in Time?

The next day at work Jerry was discussing everything that happened with one of his co-workers, Frank. Jerry told Frank about his accountant, the letters from CRA and his juicy $2,000 tax refund.

At that point, Frank interrupted Jerry and said, "Wait a minute, Jerry, your refund was only $2,000?"

Frank suggested that he and Jerry compare their tax returns because he knew they were earning the same level of salary but Frank felt like something was off with Jerry's refund.

Jerry agreed to show his tax return to Frank. As Frank was looking it over, he began shaking his head. He started to smile and then he started to laugh uncontrollably. Frank fell on the floor laughing. At this point, Jerry was very nervous and had no idea why Frank was laughing his head off.

Frank said, "Oh Jerry, good ol' Jerry, you really are such a rookie at Canadian tax, aren't you?"

"Yes, I am. That's why I have the best accountant in the world, George, to help me."

"Jerry, where are your Tuition Credits in your tax return?"

Jerry gasped. "Where are my what?"

Frank showed Jerry his tax return.

Jerry almost had a heart attack on the spot. Frank's refund was $6,000. Jerry jumped up from his seat and yelled "Frank! Your refund was $6,000! How in the world is that possible?"

Frank stopped laughing and told Jerry to calm down. He explained that every year when he was in university, he filed a tax return and claimed his tuition as a tax credit. His accountant told him that by claiming the tuition, eventually this would result in him paying less tax once he started working.

Jerry did not believe it. He never knew that he could claim tuition as a tax credit. He immediately called George and set up a meeting.

Jerry explained to George what happened with Frank and the Tuition Credits.

"Jerry, I'm so sorry, I should have realized this. I should have realized, since you were paying student loans, you obviously paid tuition and it was strange that we weren't claiming this amount in your tax return."

"Well, that's okay, it is what it is; we will just continue filing my tax returns every year and bite the bullet."

George interrupted. "Jerry, I have some good news for you. We can go back in time up to ten years and adjust your tax returns to claim any amounts you may have missed. There is nothing to worry about. I just need you to provide me with the T2202 slips from your university program for each year and I will take care of everything.

"Eventually the CRA will reassess the tax return we just filed and you will receive an additional refund. Don't forget I have to charge you a fee for all this work, of course."

Jerry was so excited to receive additional tax refunds. He wasn't excited to pay additional accounting fees for this extra work but he really didn't have a choice.

He immediately contacted his university, obtained the T2202 slips for each year and sent them to George.

Then Jerry waited. He waited and waited. He waited some more. He felt like he was waiting for a table in a busy Chinese restaurant! He continued to wait. He finally called George to ask him if he adjusted the tax returns.

George explained that he did adjust the tax returns but that it could take months or even a year or more for the CRA to process the adjustments. Jerry understood and continued to wait.

A few weeks went by and Jerry still did not hear back from the CRA so once again he followed up with George. George had no news either so he decided to call the CRA to see what was taking so long. The agent from the CRA told George that she was able to see the information submitted on the system but no specific CRA agent had been assigned to the file. The agent told George to check back in a few weeks.

A few weeks later, George called the CRA to see if they had processed the adjustments. The agent on the phone said no one had been assigned to the file yet. George was becoming frustrated and begged them to see if anything could be done to speed things up. The agent said she would submit a request to the Tax Centre to find out what was going on, but that request itself could take several weeks, so she told George to check back again in a few more weeks.

George hung up the phone, grumpy as ever. He put his head down on his desk, shut his eyes and took a short power nap.

He awakened to the sound of the phone ringing. He was hoping it would be the CRA agent with some news about the tuition adjustments.

"Hello, George speaking."

"George, any news?" It was Jerry.

Jerry asked what was taking so long for these adjustments to be processed. George updated him on the situation.

"I wish I had this money already, I could really use the extra cash to buy something extra special for Elaine. Does the CRA always take this long to process adjustments to a past year's tax return?"

"Well, it really depends. Sometimes, actually, they are very quick and the service is reasonable. But other times it can be a nightmare. It's totally unpredictable and inconsistent.

"Sometimes, when I try to call the CRA, it can take less than 5 minutes to reach a live agent on the phone. But at other times, it can take more than 30 minutes! I lose countless hours on hold trying to speak to the CRA.

"It was once reported that the Auditor General found that the service levels at the CRA can vary widely depending on where in the country you live and how friendly the CRA agent is that you are dealing with.[27] There is a 'Taxpayer Bill of Rights' that requires every taxpayer to receive the same treatment so this could be considered a violation of that right.

"One regional office can take up to 320 days to complete certain tax audits and another could take even 8 months longer than that. Adjusting a tax return can sometimes take up to 3 months or 9 months or even longer and the CRA does not have an explanation as to why that is.

"As I have told you previously, this is not the CRA's fault. The people working there are trying their best. This is the Minister of Finance's fault. The Minister of Finance needs to change the *Income Tax Act* to make the tax filing system as simple as possible. If we eliminated all tax credits and deductions, and lowered the tax rates to make up the difference, this would eliminate the need for individual taxpayers to interact with the CRA as much as we do now. It would eliminate the need for adjustments to prior year returns, CRA reviews, CRA audits, reassessments, objections and appeals.

"Anyway, Jerry, I will keep following up with the CRA regarding your adjustments and I will keep you posted."

TIP #8 — *You Can Go Back in Time*

If you were clueless about the tax system for many years and are worried you missed out on some tax deductions and tax credits, you can go back in time and adjust your tax returns for the past ten years.

This happens all the time and sometimes is a lengthy process but if you are willing to be extremely patient and if you have the documentation to prove the claims that you want to make, then you are fully entitled to file requests to adjust prior year tax returns.

These adjustments can be mailed to your Tax Centre or filed online through CRA "My Account." I have included the links to find your Tax Centre in the Resources section.

It may be worthwhile to review your past ten years of tax returns to see if you may have missed out on some credits or deductions.

Chapter 6

WHAT'S THE DEAL WITH GST CREDITS?

Jerry was doing well. His relationship with Elaine was progressing fast. They began discussing their future together. He was hoping the CRA would process the adjustments George filed because he was saving up a large amount of money to buy a surprise gift for Elaine.

One day while checking the mail, he saw another brown envelope from the CRA. He was very excited. He thought maybe this would be the tax refund from his tuition adjustments.

He opened the envelope and in large, bold letters, it said "GST Credits." The letter explained that he was eligible to receive GST Credits since his income was below a certain amount. The letter included a cheque addressed to Jerry for $90.[28] He was very happy to receive this $90 cheque but was also confused because he had no idea why he received this so he called George to find out more.

George explained to him that GST Credits are paid by the federal government to people with incomes below a certain amount to offset some of the sales tax that people pay throughout the year. Most provinces also have sales tax credits that are calculated in a similar manner so George told Jerry he could expect to receive a similar letter from the Ontario government for the Ontario Sales Tax Credit.

"George, I don't understand. Why is the government sending me cheques for GST Credits? They are taking money from every pay cheque that I receive in the form of income taxes. So if they are taking money from me, why are they giving me back tiny amounts of that money? Why don't

Please note: Numbers throughout the book have been rounded and simplified for easier readability.

they just stop taking so much money from my pay cheques in the first place and then they wouldn't need to send me GST Credits at all?"

George smiled. "Jerry, you have a lot to learn. Every aspect of our tax system has its flaws. You described this particular flaw perfectly. Your income is low enough to receive GST Credits but high enough to pay income tax. It is contradictory. If you can afford to pay income tax, then why do you need to receive GST Credits? Shouldn't the government just lower the amount of income tax you pay and then you wouldn't need them to send you these GST Credits?

"If you earn up to approximately $48,000 of income, you can receive GST Credits.[29] The amount of GST Credits you are eligible to receive decreases as your income increases. However, at an income of $48,000, you will be paying $7,000 in income tax.[30] So even if you receive $90 every three months in GST Credits, which is $360 for the year, you are still paying $7,000 in income tax. It makes no sense for the government to be paying out benefits such as GST Credits to taxpayers who are also paying income tax.

"Remember that the GST Credit system and every provincial sales tax credit system costs money to administer, and requires entire departments and bureaucracies at the CRA and Service Canada. You are going to receive these cheques from the GST Credit department every three months.

"Why can't the CRA just send you the amount of GST Credits once a year along with your tax refund, and save money on the mailing of cheques, paper and notices? Even when CRA uses direct deposit, it still costs money every time the CRA directly deposits an amount into a taxpayer's bank account."

"George, that is a great question. Why does the government send out the GST Credits four times a year? There must be a reason for that."

"My theory is that the government wants to show taxpayers how nice and benevolent it is. You will receive your provincial sales tax credits every month, which is even more extreme.[31]

"I also think there is a patronizing attitude on the part of politicians and policy makers who come up with these systems. If they sent you all the money at one time, like they do with the tax refund, perhaps they are worried you will spend it all at once and not be prudent with the funds. They don't want people wasting the money. Remember it is people with lower incomes or even zero income receiving these credits. The government does not trust these people to behave like responsible intelligent adults. In effect, they are saying, 'We can't trust you with giving you your money all in one shot once a year, even though it would save us money from an administrative standpoint. And even though you receive your tax refund in one shot, we don't trust you to receive the GST Credits in one shot.' The patronizing and inconsistent attitude of our politicians really frustrates me. Most people wouldn't even need these benefits if we eliminated income tax on the first $50,000 of income in the first place."

"Are you saying you want to eliminate GST Credits that help people with lower incomes? George, that is very cruel of you! No Canadian would ever accept such an idea."

"What I am suggesting is that the system be made more efficient all across the board. I don't want the government spending so much money to administer a bureaucratic system to transfer money to taxpayers who are also paying income tax. Just lower the rates of income tax and then a lot of people wouldn't need these credits. The funds could be re-directed to the most vulnerable people who actually do need the funds.

"The current system is ripe for abuse because people know if they show lower income, they will receive more credits from the government. If someone has a corporation they can leave their money in the corporation, show zero or very low personal income, and then receive GST Credits from the government. I actually have seen situations like this with wealthier people. Due to all sorts of factors they can show minimal personal income on their tax returns. So they file tax returns with very low or zero personal income, generating very nice GST Credit payments. The GST Credits were obviously meant to help people with low incomes, not wealthy individuals.

"Also under the current system, people are incentiveized to join the underground economy whereby people engage in cash transactions and do not report the income and therefore pay less income tax. With income tax rates so high and people receiving government benefits based on the level of income shown in their tax return, there is a clear motivation for people to show as little income as possible. The problem is when more and more people do this, the government's situation becomes less sustainable because they receive less income tax revenue but must pay out more benefits. The federal government collects approximately $35 billion in GST and then pays back $5 billion to people with lower incomes as GST Credits.[32]

"In theory, this makes sense. Canadians with lower incomes should not be burdened with paying sales tax since they are forced to spend a greater percentage of their income on purchasing the goods and services they require.

"However, practically, the system is too complicated, messy and costly to administer. Our tax dollars should be used wisely and most effectively while helping the people who need it the most. If we eliminated income tax for everyone on their first $50,000 of income, a lot of people who are currently receiving these GST Credits would no longer need them. The $5 billion currently spent on GST Credits can therefore be retargeted to the people who need it most."

Jerry said, "I never thought of it that way before. Are you suggesting that most people who receive GST Credits are paying more income tax than they are receiving in GST Credits?"

"Good question. At any level of income above $21,500 a year, people are still paying more in income tax than they are receiving back in GST Credits.[33] These people would be better off with the elimination of income tax up to $50,000 of income and then they would not need to receive their GST Credits.

"Those who earn under $13,229 per year do not pay any income tax. Those who earn between $13,229 and $20,000 usually also don't pay any income tax or pay very minimal amounts due to other tax credits that exist, such as the Canada Workers Benefit.[34] A better system than the current system of GST Credits would be to employ some sort of guaranteed minimum income."

"George, what is a guaranteed minimum income?"

"A guaranteed minimum income is when the government pays out money to those with zero income or low levels of income to ensure that these individuals will be able to maintain a basic standard of living."

"George, wouldn't giving this type of free money to people reduce their motivation to try to support themselves? How is this fair to hard-working taxpayers to have their money given to people who don't want to work?"

"Jerry, that is a fair question. There have been many different proposals regarding this idea with many different views and opinions. It is not without controversy. But the Canadian tax system already has a guaranteed income for senior citizens. Those who are 65 or older receive the tax-free Guaranteed Income Supplement if their income is less than $18,000. This is to ensure that seniors are kept out of poverty. The federal government also pays Old Age Security to senior citizens who earn income of less than $128,000[35] and pays Canada Child Benefits to those with children, as long as their family income is less than $200,000. So the federal government is already paying out $5 billion in GST Credits, $50 billion in Old Age Security and the Guaranteed Income Supplement, and $24 billion in Canada Child Benefits. That's a total of nearly $80 billion in direct transfers to individuals.

"All we need to do is take that $80 billion and re-direct it to those on the lowest end of the income scale. For example, instead of sending GST Credits to those who are earning between $21,500 and $48,000 per year, we should just eliminate income tax for these people and re-direct the freed-up GST Credit money to help those with the lowest incomes—under

$21,500. The system of Old Age Security and Canada Child Benefits should also be revamped to ensure these transfers are going to those who need it the most. Currently, these payments are going to people and families who are also paying large amounts of income tax.

"We should have a simpler system in which everyone would fall into one of three categories.

"The first category would be people with an income below $21,500 and they would be eligible to receive the guaranteed minimum income. The second category would be people with income between $21,500 and $50,000. They would not receive the guaranteed minimum income but would be exempt from paying income tax. The third category would be those with income above $50,000 and they would pay income tax on their income that exceeds $50,000.[36] This guaranteed minimum income system would replace the current inefficient and costly systems of GST Credits, Canada Child Benefits, Old Age Security and Guaranteed Income Supplement. The $80 billion currently spent on these benefits could be re-targeted as a simple guaranteed minimum income to those who need it most."

"But George, is $80 billion enough to fund your guaranteed minimum income?"

"Yes, Jerry. At least according to one estimate, this type of Guaranteed Minimum Income would cost $79.5 billion.[37] Keep in mind every province spends money on different types of support programs as well so those funds could be taken into account when re-designing this system. Look, Jerry, it's complicated and there are many different opinions on this issue and different ways of going about this.[38]

"The bottom line is that the current system, whereby people pay thousands of dollars of income tax every year yet are still eligible to receive government benefits, is just silly, inefficient and too expensive to administer.

"Jerry, just be happy you are receiving some tiny amounts of money from the government but remember you are paying them a lot more than you are receiving. Never forget that when the government gives you money in one pocket, it's usually taking more from the other pocket!"

"Wow, George, I will remember that. By the way, have you received any news about my tuition adjustments that you filed a while ago?"

"I will call the CRA right now and you can listen in on speaker."

George dialed the number. After about ten minutes on hold, he got through to a live agent.

The CRA agent said, "I can see some information was submitted and it's on the taxpayer's account but no agent has been assigned to the case yet and I can't figure out why. I suggest you re-submit all the information again and mail it to the Tax Centre instead of submitting it online."

George could not believe it. "Are you joking? Please tell me you are joking."

"Unfortunately, I'm not joking. I think you should mail in everything and that will start the process again. I'm sorry, I don't know why this happened."

Jerry and George could not believe it. Jerry felt bad that George had to do this type of work all day long. It really didn't seem like fun.

George printed off the adjustment forms and the tuition receipts and mailed everything to the Tax Centre, as the CRA agent suggested.

Jerry asked, "So George, how long do you think *this* will take? I was really counting on this money for an important purchase that could change the course of my life."

George frowned grumpily, "Anywhere from two weeks to two years."

TIP #9 — *When You Turn 19, File Your Tax Return!*

If you are 19 years or older, you are eligible to receive GST Credits from the federal government. If you know anyone who has not been filing tax returns since they were 19 years old, you should tell them immediately to go back in time and file tax returns from the year they were 19. They will receive back several hundred dollars a year, tax free. They might also receive more depending on the province they live in.

Many people think if you have zero income, you don't need to file a tax return. Technically, that is correct. However, if you have zero income, you are likely entitled to receive GST Credits and provincial credits as well so it is worthwhile to file a tax return every single year in order to receive this tax-free money.

Also, many people who are 19 years old and older have attended or will attend college or university. They should be filing tax returns and claiming the tuition as per the T2202 slips they receive each year. These Tuition Credits can be carried forward forever to offset taxes in future years. You can obtain your T2202 slip from your college or university student account online or by contacting your school. Also, in a case where you have no income, a portion of the Tuition Credits can be transferred to a parent or a spouse.

Bottom Line: If you are 19 years or older, you absolutely should be filing tax returns every year, especially if you have no income and especially if you attend college or university.

Chapter 7

Take the Bonus

One day at work, Jerry was called into the human resources department for a meeting. He was not expecting this and was naturally very nervous. To his surprise, he received some great news. He was being offered a bonus of $5,000. He was ecstatic.

He went home and realized he had almost reached his goal of saving up for that special surprise gift for Elaine. But then, it hit him. He realized this $5,000 bonus would be subject to tax and he had no idea how to calculate that amount.

He knew there were different "tax brackets" and he was worried he would be paying too much extra tax because he would be in a higher tax bracket. He wondered if it was even worth it to receive this bonus. He needed to know urgently what to do because his special surprise gift for Elaine was depending on this bonus. He called George to find out the answers to these perplexing questions.

"George, I really need this bonus. Don't tell anyone but I am planning to propose to Elaine and I am saving up money for an engagement ring. If I take the bonus, won't that push me into a higher tax bracket? Will I end up paying more tax? Is it even worth it for me to receive the bonus?"

George refused to congratulate Jerry on his engagement until Elaine actually said yes. Jerry knew George was grumpy so he didn't make an issue of it.

George chuckled at Jerry's question, "Oh, Jerry. I am so sorry this tax system is so complicated. I can't believe they do not teach the basics of our system in high school. You should always accept a bonus or a raise. Always, always, always.

"Currently, your salary is $40,000, so your after-tax income is $34,700.[39] If you take the $5,000 bonus, then your salary increases to $45,000. Some of that income will be taxed in a higher bracket, but remember it's only the additional income, above $40,000, being taxed at the higher rate. So, at $45,000 of income, your after-tax income would be $38,800.[40]

"Before the bonus, your after-tax income was $34,700. With the bonus, your after-tax income will be $38,800. So even though you pay additional tax, you are still better off after taxes."

"Phew. That's a relief. I will definitely take the bonus. Does this mean if I am offered a raise next year, I should accept the raise?"

"Yes, of course! A bonus is included in your income just like any other salary. Some people will contribute their bonuses to their RRSP so then they don't have to pay tax on the bonus, but if you need the money for that fancy ring, then that won't be an option for you. Generally speaking, the higher amount of income you earn, the more tax you will pay, but after taxes, you still have more money in your pocket so it's usually worth it to take the bonus and to accept a raise.

"Of course, there are exceptions to this rule.

"Jerry, let me tell you a story. It might shock you, but it is true, every word of it.

"I once had a client who was a hard-working lawyer in a big downtown Toronto law firm. This lawyer was happily married and had three wonderful children. He loved spending time with his family but he also felt a need to work hard and earn a big fat bonus, as he had a large mortgage to pay off, like most Canadians living in major cities.

"When it came time to receive his bonus, which was to be $25,000, the payroll department informed him that they would need to deduct $13,382 or 53.53%[41] from the bonus for income taxes. He was really upset; he couldn't believe it was that high. But because his salary for the year was over $220,000, the bonus pushed him into the highest tax bracket and the payroll department was correct.

"He said to me the following, which I will never forget. 'I can't believe it. I worked so hard for that bonus. I put in a lot of extra hours at the office, foregoing time with my wife and children. If I was to receive the whole bonus and make an extra pre-payment on my mortgage or save it for our future, it would have been worth it. But to have to pay out 53.5% of the bonus to the government, it's simply not worth it. Next year, forget about it. I will not work any extra hours. I'd rather earn a little bit less money and have more time to spend with my family.'

"You see, Jerry, once tax rates reach 50% or more, people think about that extra income differently. Even though it's true that they will be better off after taxes from a purely financial perspective, all the time, effort, energy and stress expensed to earn that extra income isn't worth it to people when they take home less than 50% of the income. Seven out of ten provinces now have a tax rate of over 50% for the highest tax bracket.[42] The problem with such a high rate is that psychologically people hit a barrier and do not want to give the government more than 50% of what they earned. So they simply will forego earning that extra income. The government therefore earns less tax revenue and everyone loses.

"Jerry, at your level of income, you don't have to worry about this. You definitely should be happy with the bonus even if some of that additional salary will be taxed in a higher tax bracket. Although your CPP and EI deductions will increase and your GST Credits that you receive will decrease, still you will be better off overall. In conclusion, please, take the bonus and be happy and go celebrate."

Jerry was very relieved to hear this advice and thanked George for his time. On his way home from work, he stopped to check the mail. There were four brown envelopes from the CRA. Jerry was hoping and praying that these were the refunds for his tuition adjustments. He slowly opened each envelope. He took out the letters and unfolded them. He couldn't understand anything on the letters so he called George again.

George said, "Jerry, congratulations! The CRA finally adjusted the tax returns to include the Tuition Credits. Each of the four letters was a reassessment for each of the tax years I adjusted. You should receive your refund cheque of $4,000 any day now, so keep checking the mail daily."

"That's great news! Thanks George, you are the best! I can't believe it took this long but you have made me a happy man."

He calculated that with the refund cheque for the tuition adjustments along with the bonus, he would be able to afford the fancy engagement ring for Elaine. He slept very peacefully that night as he planned his elaborate proposal.

TIP #10 — *Always Take Extra Income, Sometimes!*

People always say to me, "You know, I don't know what to do. If I take on this contract or take this new job or take this higher salary or sell this stock, I'm going to have to pay tax."

I always reply by asking the questioner to imagine the following scenario. Someone comes up to you and says, "Hello. Here is a cheque for $10,000. You can deposit this in your bank account but after you do, you have to send me an e-transfer for $3,000."

Now, what would you do? Would you say, "No way am I paying you $3,000."

You would have to be crazy to say such a thing.

You would take the $10,000 and gladly e-transfer back $3,000 because at the end of the day, you are ahead by $7,000.

However, if the person said to you "You have to send me an e-transfer for $9,000" you might think that perhaps it's not worth it to go to the trouble of receiving the $10,000, and giving back $9,000. Some people might think it's still worth it because at the end of the day, you are ahead by $1,000 but others might feel it's not worth the time and effort.

Senior citizens have to be careful with this issue because once they reach $79,054 of income, their Old Age Security pension begins to be clawed back and once they reach approximately $128,137 of income, they lose their Old Age Security pension entirely (for the 2020 tax year).

In terms of your specific situation, when this issue arises, you can look up the tax bracket that you are in and make an informed decision. See the Resources section at the back of the book for links to helpful tax calculators and charts showing the tax brackets. The bottom line is to remember that only the additional income you earn is taxed at the higher rate. So, after taxes, you are still better off, from a dollar and cents perspective, with the extra income.

Chapter 8

Can the CRA Just Make Stuff Up?

Jerry finally felt like he had a basic understanding of the T4 slip, the tax return and the tax refund. He also felt confident because he had George by his side. He continued working diligently at his job and he felt comfortable and secure in terms of his tax situation.

Then one evening everything changed, yet again. After eating dinner, he received a panicked call from Elaine. "Jerry, you won't believe it."

Elaine sounded calm over the phone but Jerry could hear some background noise that sounded like someone crying.

"What's wrong? Is everything all right?"

"I'm sitting here with my roommate, Pam. She received a letter from the CRA and it says she owes $25,000 of tax and if she doesn't pay up in 14 days they will continue to charge her more interest. I told Pam that she should meet with George and he should be able to fix this right up for her."

"George would definitely be able to help her. She should call George first thing in the morning. I'm sure he would appreciate a new client referral."

Elaine agreed and called George and told him about Pam and the letter from the CRA. George agreed to help Pam resolve this nasty tax situation.

Pam went to George's office for a meeting. She noticed he was very stressed out and acting in quite a grumpy manner.

George explained, "Pam, it's the middle of April. I'm in the thick of tax season. I have hundreds of tax returns to file before April 30th. Sometimes I say to myself 'serenity now!' to relieve the stress but that's not working today. Anyway, let me take a look at that letter you received."

"Thanks for taking the time to meet with me during your busy season. Jerry and Elaine speak very highly of you."

George looked at the letter and, to Pam's surprise, he didn't flinch or react in any way.

George had Pam sign an "Authorization Representative" form so he could access her CRA account online. He logged into her CRA account and was able to determine what happened within a few minutes.

"Okay, Pam, you have nothing to worry about. Here is what happened. It appears that you did not file any tax returns for the past eight years. Since you failed to file these tax returns but you did in fact have income each year, the CRA did what is known as an 'arbitrary assessment.'

"They used the tax slips they had on file for you, such as your T4, and calculated your tax return for you. They assessed 'arbitrarily' your tax returns and this has resulted in over $25,000 of taxes owing, including penalties and interest, for the past eight years."

Pam was in shock. She could not believe she would have to pay $25,000 of tax to the CRA. "But I don't understand. I thought the taxes were being deducted from every pay cheque so why would I owe $25,000 of tax?"

George looked at the Notice of Assessments for each year more closely and realized what happened. "Some years ago, it appears you had some other income that was not from employment. Perhaps it was self-employment income from a business you ran on the side?"

Pam explained to him that she did in fact, a very long time ago, do some consulting work on the side. It was only for one year. She earned about $25,000 consulting to libraries on how to make their operations more efficient.

George said to her, "The CRA used that figure and assumed every year for the past eight years you continued to earn that amount of additional income. They included that extra income in your tax return 'arbitrarily' and that is why they are saying you owe additional income tax for each of the eight years. The penalties they applied are for not filing the tax returns each year and for not paying the amounts owing on time."

Pam was very upset. "But I only earned $25,000 of self-employment income for one year, so why would the CRA assume that I had this income every year? That doesn't make any sense!"

"Of course it doesn't make sense; we are talking about Canadian tax here. When you don't file your tax returns, the CRA does it for you and estimates the amounts 'arbitrarily.' That is why they are called 'arbitrary assessments.'

"In order to fix this, I will file the actual tax returns for you based on the actual numbers. Then the CRA will reassess the tax returns correctly, remove all the balances of tax owing and they will also reverse the penalties and interest."

Pam began to calm down. "Well, I guess that's good news. So you mean I won't actually have to pay the $25,000?"

"Well, in the end, you will not. But we do need to call the collections department because the letter that you received is a 'Notice of Collection' which states that 'If the amount owing is not paid within 14 days of this letter, or a payment plan is not reached within this time, then legal action will be taken against you.'"

Pam interrupted, "Legal action? But you said I don't owe any of the $25,000 so how can they take legal action against me!?"

"Well, right now your tax account, with the amount owing, has been sent to the collections department and once it's there they have to follow strict procedures. So I will call them and explain that we are going to file all the tax returns and there will actually be tax refunds issued to you. This will ensure they don't take any further legal action against you, such as garnishing your salary or freezing your bank account."

Pam, still very confused and upset, said, "You mean they can actually garnish my salary or freeze my bank account?"

"Absolutely. They have a lot of power. In fact, I had a client, who was really sick, with cancer, for several years. He struggled to stay on top of things like filing taxes. The CRA garnished his salary even while he was on long-term disability. The CRA claimed he owed them thousands of dollars. Once all his tax returns were filed, the CRA ended up owing him back several thousand dollars. How troubling is it that his life was harder while he was sick and fighting cancer because of our complicated tax system?"

Pam could not believe this story but George insisted it was true.

George continued, "You know I remember another time I had to call the collections department to arrange a payment plan for a client. The payment plan the client proposed was not good enough because the balance they owed would have been paid in 120 days instead of 90 days. The collections agent told me I had to call the accounts receivable department to arrange a payment plan and she gave me the phone number to call.

"When I called the phone number, there was no answer. I was on hold for a while so I hung up and tried again. On my second attempt, an automated recording played that said, 'We are experiencing technical difficulties, please call again later.'

"I called back to the collections department, was on hold for another 15 minutes before reaching a live agent and told them what happened. She said to call back the accounts receivable department again the next day and their phones should be working by then. I told them that I can't sit here all day calling your phone lines praying that they are working."

Pam was surprised to hear how frustrating it can be to deal with the CRA. "George, it seems like this is a really harsh and unfair way for the government to deal with well-meaning, honest, hard-working taxpayers. What am I missing here?"

"I agree with you. The whole idea of 'arbitrary assessments' is ridiculous. It causes such inefficiency, time, effort and money to be wasted to fix these messes.

"The way the collections department deals with taxpayers creates animosity, disrespect and ambivalence, not to mention, the totally arbitrary nature of it all."

Pam was in shock after hearing all of this but she left the meeting feeling relieved that her tax situation would be rectified. She did not realize it would take many months before all her tax returns were properly reassessed and the balance owing on her account was reduced to zero.

About three months after the meeting with George, she received another letter from the CRA collections department. She called George and told him that this new letter stated that she still owed $25,000 and that legal action would be taken against her.

George told her, "Don't worry, I have spoken to the collections department and they told me to ignore those letters. They have put any collections action on hold until your tax returns are reassessed. In the meantime, because their system is automated they will continue sending out these letters to you automatically, but I can confirm that you can ignore them."

Pam was very confused, "But if they put the collections on hold, why are they still sending me letters threatening legal action? It doesn't make sense!"

"I know; you are 100% correct, but this is their system. They automatically send out letters to taxpayers who have balances owing on their tax accounts. I completely agree with you that it is outrageous and unfair that the CRA would send out inaccurate erroneous collections letters.

"In your case, due to the time lag of the CRA reassessing your returns, the amount technically is still owing even though a live agent on the phone told me the collections process is on hold but they could do nothing to stop these letters from being sent out because that is done by an automated system. It is very unfair; I agree with you; please ignore the letter."

Pam thanked George once again for his time. George hung up the phone and realized this system is so crazy. If only there was a better way!

Pam told Elaine everything that happened. Elaine couldn't believe it. She was so thankful that George was in her life. She could not imagine what things would be like without him.

TIP #11 — *File Your Tax Return on Time*

If you want to avoid the nightmare that happened to Pam, which I have seen happen on more than a few occasions in real life, you must file your tax returns on time every year. You must get serious about tax return filing and prioritize it. You must keep your tax receipts and documents throughout the year in an organized manner so you will be ready to file your tax return when the time comes. Set up an automatic reminder in your calendar just to be safe.

Filing your tax return on time every year will avoid the nightmare scenario of having the CRA arbitrarily assess your tax returns and make up balances owing that will be a long frustrating process to clear up.

TIP #12 — *Do Not Stress Over Letters from the CRA*

Many of the letters sent out by the CRA are sent out by their automated systems. Do not freak out, do not panic. Take a deep breath and try to relax.

It's very important to remain patient and calm when dealing with these issues. The vast majority of employees at the CRA want to help, are nice and well meaning. The bureaucratic mess that our tax system has become is not their fault so it's important to remember to stay calm and be polite and friendly when speaking with CRA agents.

If the CRA says they sent you a letter but you never received it, do not panic. You can request that they re-send it and confirm they have the correct address on file for you. Also, the letters they send usually show up on online mail in your CRA account. You can login to "My Account" and you will be able to see the letter there. I have seen situations where the letter doesn't actually show up in the online system but it's easy to call the CRA and request that they re-send the letter. I have listed the most common CRA phone numbers in the Resources section at the back of the book.

Chapter 9

WHY DOES THE CRA CHARGE SO MANY PENALTIES?

Jerry continued to work hard every day and pay his taxes. One day, while eating lunch in the cafeteria at work, a news story came on the television. The report described that the CRA was offering amnesty to some of the wealthiest Canadians who were clients of one of the big four accounting firms.[43] These taxpayers were caught using an offshore tax haven known as the Isle of Man, which later turned out to be a complete sham. The scheme lasted for more than a decade and involved at least $130 million.

The CRA struck a deal and promised none of these clients would be charged any penalties. The CRA alleged the scheme was "grossly negligent" and was "intended to deceive" and yet still offered amnesty to these ultra-wealthy individuals. The CRA denied any wrongdoing but the facts of the case were such that the wealthiest clients had access to and were able to afford the best tax advisors, who actively worked with the top people at the CRA to benefit their clients. The story didn't smell right and it was discovered that some top people at that particular firm and some top people at the CRA were wining and dining together.

One tax lawyer from Toronto, who represents Canadians with low and middle incomes in disputes with the CRA, said his clients are routinely dragged through the courts for years by the CRA. "It's outrageous. The CRA appears to be saying to Canadians that if you're rich and wealthy, you get a second chance, but if you're not, you're stuck."

From the CRA's perspective, they would rather settle the dispute earlier than have to go through years of court battles that would be costly. It's easier for the CRA to assess penalties and interest to those with lower incomes who don't have the resources to fight it through the courts the way Canada's wealthiest do.

Jerry could not believe it. He knew that penalties and interest were charged by CRA frequently for late-filing of tax returns and paying amounts owing late so why did the CRA offer amnesty to some of the wealthiest people in the country? Jerry had to find out more so he went to see George again.

"I saw this story too. Jerry, I fear that if I reveal to you how the system of penalties and interest with the CRA actually works, you will freak out and never want to talk to me again!"

"George, please, I want to know. Please tell me everything!"

George obliged, "Everyone knows they have to file their tax return on time and pay their taxes on time. If a tax return is filed late or a payment is made late, penalties and interest are applied by the CRA. These can often be burdensome and unfair.

"There is, of course, a method to request relief of the penalties and interest but the CRA can take up to six months or even a year to process the request, and interest will accrue daily while the CRA is processing the request. It goes without saying that many of these requests can be denied if the CRA does not accept the reason for the late filing or late payment. The taxpayer relief department must follow the guidelines that are issued from up on high. They are not permitted to relieve penalties charged to taxpayers who made an honest mistake or did not understand a particular rule. Even though our tax system is extremely complicated and it's nearly impossible to understand the rules, our tax system offers no relief of interest and penalties due to honest mistakes or misunderstandings.

"The CRA will charge a penalty of 5% for every tax return that is filed late. How do they calculate this 5% amount? The 5% is based on the amount owing on the tax return. So, if someone owed $100 of tax, they would pay a $5 penalty. No big deal, right?

"However, if someone owed $30,000 of tax for whatever reason, they would pay a $1,500 penalty. Why should the penalty for filing a tax return late be 5% of the amount owing on the tax return?

"If an employer makes a payment of payroll taxes late, they are slapped with a 10% penalty of the amount of the payment. These can really add up and most employers have to pay the payroll taxes monthly so it's easy to miss a payment due to the normal stress and hectic lives of business owners. This is very punitive and unfair.

"One cannot simply call the CRA and request the penalty be waived. One has to file a request in writing and the CRA can take up to a year to process the request and they will require proof and documentation to prove the reasons for the request being made. There is not a lot of benefit of the doubt or compassion in this system.

"If someone is charged penalties and interest on late-filed tax returns or late payments to the CRA, the interest and the penalties are not tax deductible in any way, shape or form. However, if the CRA delays paying your tax refund or amount it owes you, and they pay you interest on the amount, you must include the interest in your taxable income. The CRA is clearly double-dipping. Either the interest received from CRA and paid to CRA should be tax free on both ends or taxable on both ends. But in this case, the CRA is having their cake and eating it too."

Jerry interrupted, "George, I hate when people double dip! It's really unsanitary!"

"Yes, I agree. Double dipping is quite gross whether someone is double dipping a chip or if the CRA is double dipping in terms of interest income and interest charges.

"In recent years, the CRA implemented a Voluntary Disclosure Program whereby people who had not filed tax returns for many years or not included all their income in every tax return, because they were keeping money outside of Canada and not reporting that income, could now voluntarily come forward, disclose the income to CRA and pay the tax owing but not have to pay any penalties and interest. Of course, this mostly helped higher income and wealthier people who can afford to take extra money outside of Canada.

"Jerry, remember how those wealthy Canadians were offered amnesty on all penalties and interest on their unpaid taxes? Well you better sit down for the following story I have to tell you!"

Jerry said, "Oh great, another story!"

George continued, "A client once came to me. This client had, in a previous tax return, left out a large amount of income that was reported on a T4A slip. The CRA reassessed his tax return to include the income from his T4A slip. They sent him the reassessment with the additional tax owing, but they did not apply any penalties or interest.

"The reason they didn't apply penalties or interest is because they understood that this was the year of his retirement and he was unaware he would receive any such T4A slip since he never received one before. Since the income was on a T4A slip and the slip is automatically filed with the CRA, there is no way to hide such income.

"Unfortunately, the next year, the same thing happened again. A T4A slip was issued and this individual omitted it from of his tax return because he had no idea he would receive such a slip. The CRA decided to apply a penalty of $10,000. The amount of $10,000 was calculated as 50% of the tax owing from the extra income on the T4A slip, which was approximately $20,000. The CRA charged a 'gross negligence' penalty of 50% of the amount of tax owing because he left out this one T4A slip.

"I, of course, tried to request relief of this very unfair and punitive penalty. The argument I made was that the T4A slip is filed with the CRA automatically by the employer. It is absolutely impossible for a taxpayer to try to hide income that is already reported on a T4 or T4A slip. These slips are filed with the CRA automatically by the employer, so why would the CRA charge penalties to people for failing to leave out a T4 or T4A slip.

"A penalty of 50% of the tax owing for 'gross negligence' seemed outrageous to me. I found this so unfair and egregious that I requested a second review of the request for relief after the first request was denied. That second request was also rejected. The CRA maintained that every slip must be reported by the taxpayer because we have a 'self-reporting' tax system. I couldn't believe that the CRA can't just reassess the tax return to include all the slips they have on file. The CRA has the slip on file, and the taxpayer left it out, why not just recalculate the tax owing and forget about charging penalties. The CRA did in fact do this the first year it happened without any hassle. But because it happened again, the CRA felt it could not show any mercy or humanity!

"An honest mistake simply does not exist in the realm of our government bureaucracy. This was a 66-year-old man who worked hard and paid taxes his whole life.

"This is one of the horrible consequences of a 'self-reporting' tax system. There are huge penalties that can be applied on a whim. The current system seems to be designed for people to fail. Unfortunately, it was too late from the date when the gross negligence penalty was originally applied to file a Notice of Objection to that penalty and it would have been too costly to go to Tax Court to appeal in light of the amount of the penalty."

Jerry could not believe it. He was silent for a while and then said, "George, please tell me you have an idea of how to change this crazy system!"

George said, "Of course I do! As I told you before,[44] my dream is that the vast majority of taxpayers, who are employees, would not even have an obligation to file a tax return. There would be no potential for penalties and interest because there would be no obligation to even file a tax return!

"For those Canadians who are self-employed or have capital gains to report, they would still have to file a tax return. But even for them, I would propose that the penalties not be based on the amounts owing on the tax return. It seems arbitrary and unfair. Instead, to motivate people to file their tax returns on time, perhaps a flat rate penalty should be applied if the tax return is filed more than 30 days late. This would allow a grace period for people who are unable to file on time due to extenuating circumstances. Once 30 days passes, a modest penalty may be applied, but not by an automated computerized system. The penalty should be applied by a human being who first calls or sends a letter to the taxpayer asking why the tax return was filed late. If there was a good reason or it was an honest mistake, then that CRA agent should have the power to waive the penalty. If the CRA agent feels the penalty should apply, then the system to request relief from the penalties should be made much easier, friendlier and more transparent.

"Even if my dream does not come true, under the current system, one easy fix would be that the CRA never charge a penalty for a missing T slip. The CRA already has your T slips on file so all they have to do is reassess the tax return to include the income from the T slip. There is really no need for a penalty in such a case. No one can ever hide any income or try to evade taxes on income that is already reported on a T slip so the CRA should not charge penalties for missing T slips.

"The CRA should try to transition, as soon as possible, towards a system of 'pre-filled' tax returns whereby a person's tax return is calculated by the CRA based on all slips they have on file. Then, a pre-filled tax return would be sent to the taxpayer with a calculation of their tax refund or taxes payable. Many countries have such a system set up already and with the technology available today, there is no reason why Canada cannot move to such a system."

Jerry replied, "Well, a pre-filled tax return is better than what we have now but I'd still much prefer your idea of eliminating all credits and deductions such that we wouldn't have to file tax returns at all."

"I agree with you Jerry. In the meantime, sadly, I have more work to do." Jerry excused himself and went home, still in shock over everything he learnt. He tried to forget about what George told him because he had to prepare for a very special date with Elaine.

TIP #13 — *How to Avoid Penalties and Interest*

If you were charged penalties and interest, you might be able to request relief of the penalties and interest by filing the Form RC4288 "Request for Taxpayer Relief." You have to be very patient when filing this form as it could take a long time for the CRA to process. There must be an extenuating circumstance as to why the penalties and interest arose or as to why you are unable to pay the penalties and interest.

Remember, to avoid being charged penalties and interest by the CRA, always file your tax returns on time and, if you owe tax, always pay it on time.

If you have to pay tax in installments, set up automatic payments to come out from your bank account at the start of the year so you don't make any late payments.

Always double and triple check your tax return before filing. Whether you use Turbo Tax, UFile, H&R Block or a grumpy accountant, always look over your tax return carefully and slowly before filing to ensure you are not missing any information.

It's very important to make initial letters from the CRA a top priority. If you receive a Notice of Assessment from the CRA and wish to file an objection to the assessment, you only have 90 days—from the date of the assessment—to file the Notice of Objection. If you miss that 90-day window, you will have to file a special request to the federal Tax Court for them to give you approval to file an objection.

If you receive a brown envelope from the CRA, open it right away and send it to your tax advisor as soon as possible.

Chapter 10

LOVE AND MARRIAGE

Elaine said yes! Jerry and Elaine were very excited to begin the next stage of their life together. They could not wait to get married so they went to city hall right away and made their vows to each other and became husband and wife.

Jerry and Elaine called their trusted accountant, "George, we have some good news and bad news, and they're both the same. We got married!"

George replied, "Oh, no, you can't be serious?"

Jerry said, "That's your reaction? You can't just say congratulations? Are you really that grumpy?"

George told Jerry that both he and Elaine should come into his office as soon as possible because there was a lot to talk about regarding their tax returns.

George sat across from the happy couple in his office and was genuinely happy for them. However, he had a warning for them, "I must tell you, young lovebirds, your tax returns have become even more complicated."

"What do you mean? Now that we're married and all our finances are being combined, don't we just file one family tax return?"

George laughed and said, "What do you think this is? France? In France, families file one tax return. In the United States, there is a way for a married couple to file jointly but we're in Canada. Over here, each spouse files their own individual tax return."

Elaine said, "Well, that doesn't seem to make sense."

"Welcome to Canada."

Jerry interrupted, "Before I forget, I have to show you this letter I received from Service Canada. It says I have to pay back $180 of GST Credits. Why would I have to pay them back $180?"

George looked at the letter and explained. "Jerry, when you get married, the amount of GST Credits you are entitled to is calculated based on the combined income of you and your spouse. Now that Service Canada knows you are married, they had to demand repayment of some of the GST Credits you received after the date of marriage because from that date forward, your income was way too high to receive GST Credits since it combines your income with Elaine's income."

Jerry couldn't believe it. "But you just finished saying that we still have to file two individual tax returns even after we are married. If we have to file two individual tax returns, why wouldn't I receive GST Credits based on my individual income from my own tax return?"

"Oh, Jerry, you hear but you don't listen! This system is not logical. When you have to pay income tax to the government, the amount of tax is calculated based on your individual income. However, when the government has to pay you money, such as GST Credits, they calculate it based on your combined family income. They assume you don't really need GST Credits if you have a high combined family income.

"Of course, when they want tax from you, they do not allow you to combine income with your spouse and pay based on overall family income. The government is admitting that combined family income is a true indicator of a family's financial situation, which is why GST Credits and Canada Child Benefits are paid out based on combined family income. But the government does not allow your total family income tax bill to be based on your combined family income. It is contradictory and illogical."

"George, did you say something about children? Please don't talk about children yet."

George agreed not to talk about children until Jerry and Elaine were ready.

George continued. "To add to the confusion, some credits and deductions can, in fact, be 'shared' with or claimed by either spouse. For example, all family medical expenses can be combined and claimed on the lower-income spouse's tax return. All donation receipts can be combined and claimed on the higher-income spouse's tax return. There are quite a few other tax credits that can be claimed by either spouse, such as the first-time Home Buyers' Tax Credit, the Caregiver Credit, the Disability Tax Credit, Tuition Credits, etc. Those with certain types of pension income can split that pension income from the higher-income spouse to the lower-income spouse in order to minimize their overall income tax. So the government does allow, in some respects, spouses to share tax credits with each other to lower one's total family tax bill. But generally, your income tax bill is based on your individual income and not your combined family income."

Elaine said, "So we have to wait until we earn pension income in order to split income? We are a family unit now and already combining our income and our finances; this really seems a tad unfair."

"Well, there are other complicated ways to minimize tax as a married couple. Two such examples are spousal RRSP contributions and interest-bearing loans from one spouse to another in order to invest money. But these are fancy and complicated and beyond the scope of today's conversation. I do agree with you that most economic units are households, not individuals, and it would make more sense to tax households instead of individuals."

Elaine asked, "How much more tax will we be paying now that we are married? Are we actually going to be worse off?"

"No, you will not be worse off but you won't necessarily be better off. Jerry, your salary is now $50,000 and, Elaine, your salary is $100,000. Jerry, you will pay $7,500 of income tax[45] and, Elaine, you will pay $23,400 of income tax. Your total income tax, as a family, is therefore $30,900. But imagine a situation in which another married couple has one spouse at home not working and the other spouse earns $150,000 per year. That family will pay approximately $45,000 of income tax."

Elaine said, "Wait a minute. In both examples the total family income is the exact same at $150,000. But that other family is paying $14,100 more income tax than we are. How is that fair?"

"Well, it doesn't seem fair to me. In both cases, the family income is the same but the government has not fixed this flaw, or any flaws in the system. If you and Jerry each earned a salary of $75,000, then each of you would pay tax of $15,000 for a total of $30,000. So, as you can see, the overall family tax bill goes down as each spouse earns the same level of income."

Elaine said, "So because I am earning $100,000 and Jerry is earning $50,000, our whole tax bill is $30,900. But if we were to each earn $75,000, then our tax bill would only be $30,000. That means we are paying $900 more in tax just because I earn $100,000 and Jerry earns $50,000. That seems really unfair!"

"Exactly. Families where one spouse earns a very high salary and the other spouse earns a lower salary will be at a disadvantage when compared to a family where both spouses earn the same salary. Even though you are married, budgeting for your expenses together as a family and combining your income, for tax purposes you are considered individuals and are not allowed to have your overall family income tax bill based on the amount of your combined family income."

Jerry said, "Wait a minute, what about investment income? I have heard that many married couples split their investment income because the investments are held in a joint investment account. Can we at least split that type of income?"

"Well, yes and no. It depends. Technically, if the income earned from Elaine's job is invested, then that investment income belongs to Elaine. She cannot split that investment income with you. The only way around this problem is if Elaine would actually loan you money to invest and charge you interest. You pay the interest to her every year, which she would show in her tax return as interest income and then you could invest the money and earn the investment income in your lower-income tax bracket. You would be able to deduct the interest that you pay on your tax return."

Elaine said, "That's insane. You mean we actually have to loan each other money if we want the investment income to be recorded on Jerry's tax return? Why can't the government let us earn income and pay tax as a family unit? It would be so much simpler."

"I could not agree more. Married couples and common-law couples should be able to file one tax return as a family unit. This would make tax filing much simpler for families since there would be no need to figure out who should claim the donations, who should claim the medical expenses, who should claim this, who should claim that.

"This would also make the tax system much fairer for every single Canadian family across the board. Simplifying in this way would make a lot of tax planning for small-business owners obsolete, since they would no longer need to find creative ways of 'splitting income' with family members, which would reduce the accounting and legal bills for these small-business owners so they could keep more of their hard-earned money."

"So George, under your idea for a simple tax system, if individuals can earn their first $50,000 of income tax free, then does that mean each family would be able to earn their first $100,000 of income free of tax?"

"Well, maybe not $100,000. But it should be at least $75,000 or $80,000, due to the cost savings and economies of scale that come from living together. Similarly, a household would be eligible for the Guaranteed Minimum Income if its total income was below $30,000 or $35,000, instead of $20,000 per individual.[46]

"Each spouse would inform their employer of their total family income so their employer would be able to deduct the exact right amount of tax from each pay cheque and there would be no deductions or credits to claim. This way, there would be no need to file a tax return at the end of the year, even for families where both spouses are working."

Jerry and Elaine appreciated George's vision. They loved the idea of not having to file a tax return. They thanked him for his time and went on their merry way as they learnt more about how ridiculous the Canadian tax system is. It seemed unfair to them that other families were paying much different levels of tax than they were even though they had the same family income. But they realized there was not much they could do about it.

TIP #14 — *Communicate with Your Better Half*

The biggest problem I have seen with my married clients is a lack of communication. Granted, I am not a marriage counselor or therapist, although that might be a lot more entertaining than being a tax accountant. You absolutely must communicate with your spouse regarding your finances and taxes.

Who am I to give marriage advice? I've only been married for four years, at the time of this writing. But during the past ten years, I have filed tax returns for hundreds of married couples every year.

In my experience, usually one spouse takes care of the finances and tax return filing process. It is very important that both spouses communicate openly and freely with each other throughout the year about this topic. If donations were made or medical expenses were incurred or RRSP contributions were made and so forth, and only one spouse knows about it, then you could be leaving money on the table at tax time.

If one spouse is a disorganized type of person and the other spouse is a neat freak organizer then the neat freak organizer should be in charge of all tax documents throughout the year. The neat freak organizer should gently, kindly and calmly, without nagging, remind the disorganized spouse not to forget to keep all tax receipts. I suggest having a system using Dropbox or Google Drive to store your receipts together in one place so you will be ready to go during tax season. There are also many apps that you can download that allow you to scan in receipts directly from your phone.

Chapter 11

HOME SWEET HOME

Jerry and Elaine were outgrowing their apartment. They decided they needed more space as they knew they did eventually want to grow their family. They started to search for homes in a neighbourhood they liked. It was a stressful process but they eventually found a home they loved. After some tense negotiations, they were proud owners of a beautiful new town-house.

After they moved in, Jerry called George to tell him that they moved and informed him of their new address.

"Jerry, congratulations on your new home. I will keep your new address on file but I have some bad news for you."

"Oh no, what is it this time, George?"

"Well, I cannot change your address with the CRA on your behalf. You need to do this yourself. This is for security reasons, so this is one tax policy that actually makes sense, if you can believe that! You can change your address with the CRA online through the 'My Account' portal."

Jerry breathed a sigh of relief, "Thanks, George. That was not as bad as I thought it would be."

George said, "Did you take out money from your RRSP under the first-time Home Buyers' Plan to help with the down payment?"

"Yes, I did. I withdrew $35,000 actually. Will that be a problem?"

"No, it's not a problem. But you will need to repay $2,333 ($35,000 divided by 15) back into your RRSP each year for the next 15 years. Or, instead of repaying the money into the RRSP, $2,333 will be included in your income in your tax return for each of the next 15 years."

"Okay, that doesn't seem so bad. Is there anything else I need to know?"

"Of course there is! We will need to claim the first-time Home Buyers' Tax Credit on your tax return and I hope you claimed a rebate for first-time home buyers of the land transfer tax."[47]

"Okay, George, let's make sure to claim that first-time Home Buyers' Tax Credit. And, yes, my real estate agent and real estate lawyer who did the closing on the house knew I was a first-time home buyer and they assured me the rebate for land transfer tax was claimed."

George smiled to himself. "Good job Jerry, you are getting good at this tax stuff. Now I must warn you of one more issue that many people are unaware of."

Jerry was nervous. He listened intently.

"Jerry, when you sell the house in the future, you must tell me at once. There is a new rule that requires anyone who sells their house to declare it in their tax return in the year that the house is sold."

Jerry's jaw dropped. "What are you talking about? Elaine and I will be living in the house. Doesn't that mean it's our 'principal residence'? I thought we don't pay tax when we sell the house that we are living in? George, say it ain't so!"

"I understand it's your principal residence because you will be living there. You must still declare the fact that you sold the house in your tax return. There will be zero tax to pay because it is in fact your principal residence, so you have nothing to worry about in that respect. But even though there is no tax to pay, you must now declare the sale of your principal residence in your tax return."

Jerry was relieved there would be no tax to pay. "If there's no tax to pay, why do I need to report the sale of my principal residence? Does the government need to know every move I make?"

"Yes, they do! They are worried about people flipping properties and declaring the sale of these properties as their principal residences or not claiming them at all. So, to clamp down on property flippers and real estate investors trying to evade tax, the government is now requiring every single sale of every single property to be disclosed. Like I said, there will be no tax to pay so you have nothing to worry about."

"George, what if Elaine and I decide to rent out the basement to earn some extra income to help pay down the mortgage? Are we allowed to do that?"

"Yes, you are definitely allowed to rent out a part of your house. But you must be careful here. If you rent out half or more of the house, or if you need to make significant structural changes to the house to be able to rent it out, then you might jeopardize your principal residence status."

"So you mean, as long as we don't do renovations in order to rent it out, and assuming we only rent out a small part of the house, then we are okay?"

"Yes, exactly. When you sell the house, it will be tax free if you are only renting out a small part of the house and you weren't required to do major structural changes. Also, you cannot claim 'capital cost allowance,' otherwise known as depreciation, which is an expense that represents the decrease in value of the building over time."

"Okay, that's amazing. Thanks, George. Tax-free rental income, here we come."

George gasped.

"Everything okay, George?"

"Why do you think the rental income will be tax free?"

"Well, we are merely using the extra cash earned from the rent to pay our mortgage off. Are you saying we still have to pay tax on this income?"

"Of course. You must pay tax on every dollar of income. You are allowed to deduct expenses against the rental income to lower your tax bill. You can claim a portion of the property taxes, home insurance, mortgage interest and repairs and maintenance. If you pay utilities for your tenant, then you can claim a portion of that as well. So the net income, after expenses, might not amount to much, but you still have to pay tax on that net income."

Jerry became a bit sad after learning all this but he thanked George for explaining everything. He went home and updated his address through his CRA "My Account" portal online. He told Elaine she would have to update her address on her CRA account as well because Jerry could not do it for her. Elaine laughed at the inefficiency of this but obviously had no choice but to comply.

TIP #15 — *You Must Report the Sale of Your Home in Your Tax Return and More*

You will not pay tax when you sell your principal residence but it must absolutely be reported on Schedule 3 of your tax return in the year that you sell the house. Failing to report this can result in onerous penalties so please do not forget this and tell everyone you know that they must report the sale of their home in their tax return.

If you are withdrawing funds from your RRSP under the Home Buyers' Plan to purchase the house, remember you have to repay the amounts back into your RRSP for the next 15 years. If you don't have the money to repay into your RRSP, you can include the amount that must be repaid as income in your tax return each year.

Don't forget to claim the first-time Home Buyers' Tax Credit if you are, in fact, a first-time home buyer. If you are married, and your spouse is not considered a first-time home buyer, even if you are, then you cannot claim the first-time Home Buyers' Tax Credit.

If you rent out a portion of your home to a long-term tenant, the rental income must be reported on the T776 Statement. The link to this statement is included in the Resources section.

If you rent out a room or portion of your home for short-term rentals, such as Airbnb, then this must be reported as income on the T2125 Statement of Business or Professional Activities form. If you reach $30,000 of revenue from such short-term rental income, you will have to register for GST (see Chapter 15, The Hardship of Being a Self-Employed Tax Collector).

Chapter 12

CHILDREN—LITTLE BUNDLES OF TAX BENEFITS

Jerry and Elaine continued their busy lives, working hard and paying their taxes. They settled into their new home and decided it was time for them to give birth to new little future taxpayers. Jerry remembered George said something about tax benefits relating to children so he set up a meeting to ensure he wouldn't miss out on any free money from the amazing government.

George congratulated Jerry and Elaine on their upcoming bundle of joy. He reminded Elaine she should apply to receive maternity benefits from EI. "If you are going to be taking time off work to have a child you can apply to receive maternity benefits from Service Canada. Remember how you had 'EI'—Employment Insurance—deducted from your pay cheques? Well, all those EI contributions go into a fund that pays out benefits to people who need to go on sick leave, get laid off from their jobs or take time off work to have children."

Elaine said, "Okay, sounds splendid."

"Well, sure. Remember it will take you at least an hour to fill out the application. Once you start receiving the benefits, remember that they are taxable. Taxes will be deducted from the benefits and when you file your tax return you may or may not have more tax to pay from receiving this income."[48]

Elaine said, "You mean I have to pay tax on my maternity benefits?"

George explained to her that, yes, she did have to pay tax on EI benefits.

Please note: Numbers throughout the book have been rounded and simplified for easier readability.

He also told her the amount of EI benefits she receives is included in the family net income calculation that is used to calculate the amount of Canada Child Benefits they will be entitled to.

"What are Canada Child Benefits?" she wondered.

George explained to them that they needed to apply for the Canada Child Benefit once their child is born. "The Canada Child Benefit is money the government sends you for having kids. They calculate the amount you are going to receive based on your combined family net income."

Jerry and Elaine said, "That's great, free money from the government!"

George said, "Not exactly! Remember you and Jerry are paying approximately $30,900 of income tax every year. That's where this Canada Child Benefit money comes from. The government is returning a small amount of money back to you that you already paid in income tax.

"Also, remember this is another great example of government double dipping. When it comes to calculating the taxes you have to pay, the government calculates that number based on each of your individual incomes separately. But when they pay you your child benefits, they combine your family income together and use that amount to calculate how much you are entitled to receive."

"Okay, so it's not perfect but so long as I receive my benefits, I won't complain."

"Everyone says that and that's why we have this crazy system. Remember these benefit programs cost money to administer and sometimes it can take a long time for people to receive the benefits they are entitled to. Hopefully that won't happen to you."

Jerry and Elaine were thankful for the information and applied for maternity benefits. It took Elaine a while to fill out the application but after a couple of hours it was complete and a few weeks later, she began to receive her benefits. She appreciated that she could receive EI before her child was born since she began her maternity leave early.

A couple of months later, their little new tax benefit generator was born! He was a healthy little boy and they were overjoyed. They decided to name him Soda. They applied to receive the Canada Child Benefits just as George suggested. Sometime later, they received a letter from Service Canada that said they would begin receiving the monthly amount of $120.[49] They were very happy. Although it wasn't much considering how much income tax they paid, it was nice to get a little something back.

Elaine called George. "George, thanks for letting me know about the Canada Child Benefits. We received the letter informing us that we would soon be receiving the payments monthly. Oh, and by the way, you gotta see the baby. He's breathtaking." George promised he would make a point of going to visit to meet the new baby.

As time went on, Jerry and Elaine had two more children. For each child, they went through the process of applying for maternity benefits and Canada Child Benefits. They felt like they were experts now.

Eventually, Elaine decided she wanted to work two days less a week to be able to spend more time with their children. She was unsure if she could afford to do this because it would mean a reduction of $40,000 from her annual salary of $100,000.

Jerry and Elaine agreed to consult with George to see what he thought.

Elaine said, "I really want to stay home and take care of the kids instead of working so hard. Even if I could reduce my hours and work part time, I feel like this would be easier for me and more in line with the lifestyle I want right now while my children are young. But Jerry and I are really worried about our income. If I work two days less a week, I will lose $40,000 in salary. I just don't think we will be able to make that work. What do you think, George?"

George said that this was an amazing question and he has been asked this before many times. He told them, "Currently, with three kids, and both of you working full time, your annual total tax bill is $30,900 and annual total Canada Child Benefits are $6,400. So your total after-tax income is $150,000 minus $30,900 plus $6,400 which is equal to $125,500.

"Now, if you were to work two days a week less, then your salary would decrease from $100,000 to $60,000. So in this scenario you would earn a total family income of $110,000, including Jerry's $50,000 salary. Your total family tax bill would be $19,000, and you would receive Canada Child Benefits of $9,200. Therefore, your family's after-tax income would be $100,200.

"So when we take into account the decrease in taxes as well as the increase in Canada Child Benefits, you are actually only losing out $25,300, not $40,000."

Jerry and Elaine could not believe it. They now knew the truth that George was a magical wizard with unlimited powers. They realized that they would be able to make things work if she stayed home two days a week because the reduction in salary was a lot less painful taking into account taxes and the increase in Canada Child Benefits.

George said to them, "This is actually very smart and logical. You, like all human beings, are responding to incentives. You realize that by working less, although your gross income from your salary will decrease, you know that after taxes the decrease will not be as much as it seems. And you also know that because your income will be decreasing, along with the fact that you have three children, the Canada Child Benefits that you will receive will increase substantially. This is a perfect example of the strange incentives the Canada Child Benefit system creates.

"If the government wants to help Canadian families and give them money, all it has to do, very simply, is to stop taking so much of their money in the form of income taxes! Remember, the majority of Canadians who receive Canada Child Benefits are also paying income tax.

"It makes no sense for the government to take money from people and then give some of it back. A much simpler solution would be to eliminate income tax for people who earn below $50,000, as I have suggested before,[50] and then most of these benefits would be unnecessary. A simpler system would also save taxpayers billions of dollars in administration costs at Service Canada and the Canada Revenue Agency. Additionally, people with higher incomes, such as yourselves, don't really need the Canada Child Benefit. All you need is a reduction in income tax. When you really think about it, the Canada Child Benefit is merely a tax-free refund of some of your income tax. Remember, you are paying $30,900 annually in income tax and receiving back $6,400 in Canada Child Benefits. So, for the sake of simplicity, why not just reduce income tax and then there would be no need for the Canada Child Benefit for many people. The money being sent to people with higher incomes under the current system could then be redirected to those on the lowest end of the income scale as part of a simple Guaranteed Minimum Income."[51]

"George, many people rely on these monthly cheques or deposits into their bank accounts. I don't understand how you can be so cruel and heartless in proposing to eliminate the Canada Child Benefit!"

"Jerry, the Guaranteed Minimum Income could replace the current systems of GST Credits, Canada Child Benefits, Old Age Security and Guaranteed Income Supplement. The funds being paid out for these systems could be re-directed to those who need it most.

"In 2018-2019 there were approximately 1.5 million families with net incomes of $75,000 or more who received Canada Child Benefits totaling $5.7 billion.[52] These families would be better off with the elimination of income tax on the first $50,000 of income.[53] For example, a family where one spouse earns $50,000 and the other spouse earns $25,000 will pay $9,600 in income tax.[54] This family, assuming they have two children under the age of six, will receive Canada Child Benefits of $7,301. So this family would be better off without receiving Canada Child Benefits, along with an elimination of income tax on the first $50,000 of income per individual, or $75,000 per household.[55] Then, this $5.7 billion could be redirected to those on the lowest end of the income scale, as part of the Guaranteed Minimum Income.

"One of the main problems with the Canada Child Benefit system and all the other benefit systems as they currently exist is the administrative hassle involved in ensuring these benefits are being paid out correctly.

"In fact, it's estimated that Canadians are missing out on $1.2 billion of benefits annually, such as GST Credits, Canada Child Benefits, Guaranteed Income Supplement and others, because they either don't know about these benefits, don't know how to apply for them or feel that the forms are too complicated to fill out and not worth their time."[56]

George continued—he was on a roll now. "A CBC report detailed how every year the CRA sends out 350,000 letters to Canadians letting them know that their eligibility for certain benefits is being reviewed.[57] The report described how single parents especially get targeted by these reviews in order to prove that they have custody of their children and the results cause 'anxiety, humiliation and anger.' Some taxpayers reported the CRA didn't give them enough time to gather the necessary proof, and that the documentation the CRA required was too difficult to put together. Many were embarrassed that they would have to go to the school, doctor, employer, landlord, etc., and explain their marriage and financial situation. Many also told the focus group they're still frustrated by their inability to get anyone from CRA on the phone.

"A single dad of two sons in Kitimat, BC, told the interviewer that he's had to fight the CRA for countless months over more than $2,000 in child benefit payments that he said he needs to pay his bills. He has had his hydro disconnected twice and his attempts to sort it out over the phone with the CRA have been fruitless. 'I just keep getting the runaround. They put up all this red tape so you get frustrated and give up,' he said.

"A single mom in Saskatoon with five children under the age of 12 explained that she never received the first review letter and then, without warning, lost all her benefits. The CRA even said she owed $18,000! She eventually got her benefits back and her bill reversed but not until she was able to get a dedicated CRA case worker who made the unusual decision to allow her friends to give telephone interviews attesting to her separated status.

"An Auditor General's report of a year ago showed major problems with the CRA's call centres and the accuracy of the information the CRA was providing to taxpayers. Concerns that Canada continues to let big tax cheats hide money in tax havens continue to grow, all the while the CRA goes after single parents to determine their eligibility for Canada Child Benefits. All these findings have some opposition MPs calling on the government to make major changes to the way the CRA conducts itself and who it goes after.[58]

"Sorry. Our crazy tax system makes me a little *crazy*. Sometimes I need to get it out."

Jerry and Elaine were in shock. Although it was so nice they were receiving Canada Child Benefits, they couldn't help but realize how bizarre it was that it made more sense for Elaine to work less and earn more taxpayer-funded benefits.

After all, if more and more taxpayers made that decision, then overall tax revenue would decrease dramatically, while, at the same time, the benefits that the government pays out would increase. Clearly, this was not a sustainable system due to the strange incentives it creates.

Jerry and Elaine left George to continue his work and they now could understand why George was so grumpy. They became a bit grumpy themselves as they learnt more and more about how complicated the tax system was as they grew older and wiser.

TIP #16 — *Apply for Everything*

When you make the fateful decision to bring new lives into this world, ensure you apply for everything you are entitled to receive as a reward from our wonderful government. To apply for EI maternity benefits, you will need your Record of Employment (ROE) from your employer. You can apply for EI maternity benefits online by setting up a My Service Canada Account. The link to this is provided at the back of the book on the Resources pages.

Remember that the EI benefits you receive are taxable so it's possible when you file your tax return at the end of the year that you may actually have a small balance of tax owing.

You should apply for Canada Child Benefits once your child is born. The links for this online application are in the Resources section as well.

Chapter 13

KIDS ARE EXPENSIVE; GOVERNMENT IS HERE TO HELP, OR ARE THEY?

Jerry and Elaine's children were now toddlers running around everywhere. Up until now, they were lucky enough to have their parents watching the kids three days a week so they could both concentrate on their work. But the grandparents no longer had the energy to deal with the kids anymore. Elaine decided she needed to hire a nanny at once. She had fond memories of her childhood nanny back in England.

Elaine had read in the news about the "child care deduction" so she knew there would be some tax consequences of this decision. She set up a meeting with George to make sure she was doing everything properly.

"George, I need a nanny badly," Elaine said. "Jerry's parents can no longer watch my insanely active, highly energetic children. Can we claim the cost of hiring the nanny as a deduction on our tax return?"

"Yes, of course, but only the lower-income spouse can claim it. So Jerry will be able to claim that on his tax return, and this will increase his tax refund."

Elaine was so happy. "That's amazing. Please claim the payments we make to our nanny on our next tax return. I will send you the total amount at the end of the year. I will now go and begin the search for a suitable nanny."

George shook his head, "Not so fast Elaine, do you really think it will be that easy? You are becoming an employer. You will need to register for a payroll account with the CRA. Additionally, you will need to calculate the proper CPP, EI and income tax deductions from the caregiver's pay. You will need to provide a proper legal pay stub every time you pay the nanny. You will need to match her CPP contribution and pay 1.4 times her EI contribution from your own pocket. You will need to pay all the taxes deducted from her pay along with your employer portion to the CRA by the 15th of each month (or quarterly if you have perfect compliance) and you will need to file a T4 each year. And if your caregiver stops work, you will need to provide a record of employment."

Elaine's heart sank. "Are you serious? You mean I can't just pay her? I have to go through all that bureaucracy? Surely you can't be serious?"

"I am serious, and don't call me Shirley. Don't worry, Elaine, I will take care of everything for you, but sadly I will need to increase my fee for all this extra work. There are other options such as payroll service providers that will do everything for you but they charge a hefty monthly fee. I can send you some links to those services."

Elaine said, "You know I trust you. Let's just get it done. I just can't believe how much work is involved in hiring even one employee. Will the government compensate me fairly for all this work I am doing for them?"

George burst out laughing at that question.

"Sorry, Elaine. I don't mean to laugh at you but do you really think the government compensates employers for all the work involved in complying with the CRA's requirements for payroll? What kind of dream world are you living in? The government is able to collect taxes from Canadians only because employers expend great time, effort and costs in order to calculate the payroll source deductions of their employees and comply with very difficult, complicated and unforgiving deadlines, due dates and filing requirements. Oh, and before I forget, if there is any period of time in which you have no employees but still have a payroll account registered, you must actually file 'nil remittances.'"

"What is a nil remittance?"

"Well, it means you have to inform the CRA payroll department that you are not paying any payroll for the period in question. It's quite bizarre when you think about it. Even when you have no obligation to make any tax payment or tax filing, because you had no employees for a certain period of time, the CRA must be informed of this by way of a 'nil remittance.' Bureaucrats must always know what's happening with your business, even if nothing is happening.

"It's a tax return about nothing!"

Elaine was now quite fearful of the idea of being an employer but relaxed knowing she had George by her side to guide her. She thanked George for his time and George registered the payroll account for her. Elaine then began the search for a caregiver for her children. Eventually the search proved to be fruitless and she changed her mind and decided to send her youngest child to a day care instead.

Months went by and one day Elaine saw a brown envelope in the mail from the CRA. It had a very scary letter from the CRA payroll department. It was an audit. Elaine was terrified; she began trembling with fear. She immediately called George and told him the contents of the letter.

The letter said that the CRA requested to see her last 12 months of bank statements, cancelled cheques and many other documents. They were asking for her accounts receivable listing, accounts payable listing, sales listing and so forth. It seemed to be a full audit for a business but she had never run a business in her life. She had no idea why they would be doing this. George looked into it and called the phone number listed on the CRA audit letter.

The CRA agent on the phone told George that a payroll account was opened but there was never any activity on the account. The letter Elaine received was generated automatically by the system whenever a taxpayer sets up a payroll account and opts to remit payroll tax payments quarterly. Since the quarterly option was chosen, the CRA audit department automatically sent the letter. She explained it was not really an audit but rather just a service they were providing to her to ensure her business was being set up properly right from the beginning and to ensure she knew her payroll obligations.

George was flabbergasted. He explained to the agent that she does not have a place of business; she is simply a mother who thought she would hire a nanny and then changed her mind. The payroll account was opened, but never used, and she would like to close down the payroll account at this time.

The agent on the phone didn't really know how to respond, so George asked to speak to a supervisor. The supervisor was very helpful and allowed George to close down the payroll account without going through the whole audit process.

George decided to take some action against this out-of-control bureaucracy. He filed a "service complaint" and explained in his complaint that it is outrageous that CRA audit exam letters are sent out automatically to every taxpayer who opens a payroll account as a quarterly remitter.

The politicians and academics who come up with these policies do not understand how much of a hassle it is and how scary it can be for a normal average human being to have to go through these exams and read these audit letters. The payroll letter that Elaine received actually said "If you do not respond to this and provide the required documentation, legal action may be taken against you without further notice."

George was so frustrated with the way the government was dealing with taxpayers. Elaine also could not believe how much bureaucracy she had to deal with without even hiring a nanny. She could not begin to imagine how much work it would have been to actually hire, pay the nanny properly, pay the taxes properly, file the T4 properly and so forth. She was thankful she opted to send her child to a day care instead.

TIP #17 — *Stay Up to Date, Keep Keeping Receipts, Get Help*

I said it before and I'll say it again. The slew of tax credits and deductions changes every year. So to ensure you are getting every possible dollar back on your taxes from every tax credit you are entitled to, you need to stay up to date. Do proper research, read the news or work with a competent tax advisor or accountant who will stay up to date for you.

If you pay for child care expenses, keep all receipts! Always keep the receipts, never not keep the receipts, and remember to keep the receipts. Did I mention to keep all your receipts?

The child care deduction can be very valuable so it's important not to forget about it. Remember it can only be claimed by the lower-income spouse and only if that lower-income spouse is working and has employment income or self-employment income.

If you are a family in which one spouse does not earn any employment or self-employment income, you will not be able to claim the child care deduction. There is an exception if the spouse staying home has a disability or is in post-secondary education full time.

Lastly, if you are going to hire a caregiver, such as a nanny, for God's sake, please do not try to calculate the payroll deductions and get it set up on your own. It is a bureaucratic nightmare and if you make one payment late to the CRA for the payroll taxes, you will be charged a 10% penalty of the amount of the payment. Being an employer can be an unforgiving bureaucratic mess so please make sure you get proper advice and help right from the beginning of the process.

Chapter 14

HOW TO SAVE MONEY

Jerry and Elaine continued to work hard, save money and experience a lot of pleasure in watching their kids excel at elementary school. Their eldest child, Soda, was only seven years old, but he already knew he wanted to become a doctor. Jerry and Elaine were thrilled but they were nervous about the costs and debt he would incur from university and medical school.

Jerry had seen a lot of advertisements for these strange creatures known as RESPs, RRSPs and TFSAs. He vaguely knew what an RRSP was because he had been contributing to it for a long time and withdrew some money from his RRSP to help fund their house purchase. He decided to call George and find out more.

George began, "Jerry, if you want to put away money for your children's college or university, then the account you are looking for is the RESP. This is the 'Registered Education Savings Plan.' You go to your bank and tell them you want to open an RESP account. Once it's open, you can put money into the RESP, invest it and then all that investment income you earn will be tax free.

"When your child starts college or university, you take out money from the RESP. The money taken out will be shown as income on your child's tax return. If your child is working as well as going to school at the time, the RESP withdrawal amount will be added together with their other income and taxes would be paid on it. But most college or university students are typically not in high tax brackets so the income would be taxed at fairly low rates."

Jerry said, "Okay, that sounds pretty good. I saw some advertisements for these group RESPs with a lot of fine print, what's the deal with those?"

"Stay far away Jerry, far away from those. Those can have very high fees and people who try to withdraw money early from those plans get penalized because they don't read the fine print. Instead of those, simply go to your bank and tell them you'd like to open an RESP. I suggest opening a family RESP so it automatically includes all your children as beneficiaries."

"Thanks, George, I will go ahead and do that. How much money can I put in?"

"You can put in a maximum of $50,000 for each child over the lifetime of the account. Every year, if you put in $2,500, the government will match it up to $500. So it's definitely a no brainer to put in at least $2,500 per year per child if you are able to."

"What do you mean the government matches up to $500?"

"This is known as the 'Canada Education Savings Grant.' It's a nice small way the government helps people to pay for their college or university. Remember, Jerry, you are paying tens of thousands of dollars in tax every year, so be grateful the government is giving a tiny bit of that back to you."

Jerry promised that he was indeed grateful for this. He told George he would open a family RESP as soon as their meeting was finished but he had another question.

"Elaine and I have been doing well over the past number of years. I paid off my student loans, we pay our credit cards in full every month and the only debt we have is our mortgage. We've even managed to save up a bit of cash in our bank account by being careful over the years. But we have no idea what to do with this money. We've already been making the maximum amount of RRSP contributions. Is there anything else we can do with this money?"

"Jerry! Why don't you put this in a TFSA?"

Jerry said, "You have to explain to me what a TFSA is?"

George said, "Don't you read the news? Must I tell you everything?"

Jerry said, "Um, hello? Isn't that your job?"

George sat back in his seat and sighed. "Jerry, our tax system is so complicated. Even something as simple as saving money for your future has become a maze that is very difficult to figure out. Let me explain from the beginning.

"First, I'm glad you've been contributing to your RRSP. The RRSP is the Registered Retirement Savings Plan. When you contribute money into your RRSP, you are allowed to deduct the amount of your contribution on your tax return. Therefore, your taxes payable decreases so you end up usually getting a nice tax refund."

Jerry interrupted, "Yes George, I love my tax refunds. Every year we spend most of the money, but do manage to save a bit from each refund."

"Saving never hurt anyone, so I'm very proud of you in that regard. Now, with the RRSP, the idea is to make contributions and claim them on your tax return during your working years when you have a nice high income and pay a lot of tax. That way, it generates nice big juicy tax refunds. Then, when you retire, and your income is probably going to be a lot lower, you can take out the money from the RRSPs. The money you take out from the RRSP is shown as income on your tax return and you have to pay tax on it. But since you are in retirement and presumably at a lower level of income, you pay a lower rate of tax at that time.

"So it's a win-win because you receive the tax refunds during your working years that you can use to pay down debt or put in your kids' RESPs or otherwise save. The money within your RRSP earns investment income tax free as long as you don't withdraw from the RRSP. Then, when you retire, you pay a low rate of tax when the money comes out of your RRSP to fund your retirement."

Jerry said, "Wow, George, it sounds amazing. I will tell everyone I know to contribute to their RRSP."

George interrupted, "Wait, Jerry, you have to be careful. There are some disadvantages of the RRSP. If someone is in a low tax bracket throughout their working life, the RRSP might not make sense. The tax refund might be very small in such a situation so the TFSA, which I will explain, might be a better option for such an individual.

"Also, you must be very careful because when you turn 71 years old, you can no longer contribute to your RRSP. Instead, minimum amounts are required to be withdrawn from your RRSP and these withdrawals are included in your income on your tax return every year until you die. So if you end up being in a very high tax bracket in those years, you could end up paying very high rates of tax.

"Last, if you have debt, there is an age-old debate about the question of whether you should pay down debt or contribute to your RRSP. If the debt has very high interest rates, such as credit card debt, it's better to pay down that type of debt. If the debt has lower interest rates, like the mortgage on your home,[59] then it may be more beneficial to contribute to your RRSP and invest the money rather than making prepayments on your mortgage."

Jerry said, "So it's not simple after all. Why is this so complicated?"

George frowned, "I just don't know Jerry. Every single Canadian is forced to hire people like me and other financial planners and advisors to figure out how to best save for their future. It is a very complicated system and not easy to figure out. The bottom line is try to save some money from each pay cheque, put it away in an RRSP or a TFSA or even both, if you can."

Jerry interrupted, "Wait, what is a TFSA?"

"Oh, right. The TFSA is the 'Tax-Free Savings Account' and it was created in 2009. The TFSA is what you should be putting all that cash sitting in your bank account into. Take that cash, open a TFSA, put the money in there. Then, invest the money within your TFSA and all the investment income will be tax free."

"George, how much money can I put into the TFSA?"

"Good question. If you were 19 years old—or older—in 2009, then you would have $5,000 of contribution room for the years 2009 through 2012, $5,500 for 2013 and 2014, $10,000 for 2015, $5,500 for 2016 through 2018 and $6,000 for 2019 and 2020, for a total of $69,500. See how complicated this is? The amount is supposed to rise over time with inflation in increments of $500.

"That's a lot money. So what's the difference between the TFSA and RRSP? They sound like they are exactly the same!"

"That's a great question. When you put money into your TFSA you are not able to deduct that amount on your tax return so you do not get a tax refund. On the flip side, when you take money out of your TFSA, you do not have to show that amount as income on your tax return and you do not pay tax on the withdrawal. So it is much more flexible than an RRSP because you can take money out without paying tax on it."

"Okay, so which one is better? The RRSP or the TFSA?"

"That's a very good question. There is no right answer; it really depends on every individual's specific situation. Here are some rules of thumb. If you have enough money to maximize both your RRSP and your TFSA, then go ahead and maximize both.

"If you only have enough money to maximize one, if you are in a high-income tax bracket while you are working, then the RRSP might be the better option. You can take the tax refund from the RRSP contribution and put that into your TFSA. If you are in a low-income tax bracket, the TFSA is probably a better option.

"If you know you need the money in the next few years, then the TFSA might be a better option since withdrawals are tax free. Oh, and Jerry, if you go blabbing to people about our conversation make sure that if you speak to any Americans who live in Canada, they know that this advice does not apply to them and they should talk to an American accountant. It's usually not a good idea for Americans who live in Canada to have a TFSA.

"Jerry, as you can see, it's very complicated and there is no one right answer for everyone."

Jerry said, "Yes, it definitely seems insanely complicated. So what do you recommend for Elaine and I?"

"Well, I recommend you and Elaine open the family RESP for your children to help save for their college and university and put in at least $2,500 per year per child if you are able to. Keep making those RRSP contributions. You and Elaine should each also open a TFSA account and take all that cash sitting in your bank account and put it right into the TFSA.

"Be careful not to deposit more than you are allowed to. There is a maximum amount you are allowed to contribute into the RRSP, RESP and TFSA so you have to be careful. You can be charged penalties if you put too much money in."

"George, thank you so much for the advice. I will definitely open the RESPs for my children and we will continue contributing to our RRPSs but the TFSAs seem like overkill so I will pass on those."

George jumped up from his chair and screamed, "George is getting upset! Jerry, are you out of your mind? Do you realize how valuable the TFSA is? Imagine you are 19 years old and you contribute $6,000 to your TFSA every year for 46 years, until you turn 65. Furthermore, imagine you earn a return in your TFSA of 5% every year. Remember, the income earned within the TFSA is tax free. Guess how much money you will have in the TFSA once you turn 65?"

"George, I have no idea. I'm not a numbers guy. Just tell me, don't leave me in suspense."

"Jerry, you will have $1,000,000 in your TFSA when you turn 65."
"Whoa!"

"That's right. And the money you withdraw from your TFSA in retirement is tax free and is not included in income in terms of calculating what other benefits you are entitled to, such as Old Age Security and the

Guaranteed Income Supplement. I absolutely insist and urge you to contribute to your TFSA each year as much as you possibly can. Also, keep in mind, the TFSA contribution room keeps increasing every few years or so due to inflation. You do not want to miss out on this."

Jerry relented, "Fine George, you win. I will go to the bank with Elaine and we will each open a TFSA account."

Jerry could not believe how complicated saving money was. RRSPs, RESPs, TFSAs. He and Elaine went to the bank together and opened all the accounts. It took more than two hours of filling out what felt like endless amounts of paperwork. They were relieved when it was all finally completed. They called George to tell him the good news.

George said, "Elaine, Jerry, you will not regret opening those accounts. I'm very happy you followed my recommendations. It was the right thing to do. I wish there were a simpler way for people to invest and save money. Instead of RRSPs, TFSAs and RESPs, there must be a better way to encourage people to save money without all the complicated, confusing and inefficient rules regarding these accounts."

Jerry cut him off, "George, we are exhausted. We would love to hear your ideas about making the system simpler, but for now, we are going straight to bed to recover from today's encounter with the complexity of the Canadian tax system."

TIP #18 — *Max Out Your Registered Accounts*

If you have wads of cash lying around in a chequing account or savings account and you have no idea how to save it, the first step is to contribute it to your registered accounts. Even if you have small amounts to invest and save, every dollar makes a difference. Large or small, it's important to ensure you are using these "registered" accounts as much as possible.

RRSPs and TFSAs are known as "registered" accounts which means once the money is in the account, the investment income that is earned within those accounts is not subject to income tax. When money is withdrawn from the RRSP, it is included in one's income in the year of withdrawal, so technically, the RRSP is more of a tax-deferral vehicle.

"Non-registered" accounts are investments that are held outside of your RRSP or TFSA.

It is simple common sense that you should first ensure these registered accounts are maxed out before having other investments that are not in these accounts.

The tax savings, over your lifetime, can be enormous by having your money in the RRSP and TFSA accounts as opposed to non-registered accounts, due to the compounding effect of having tax-free income being re-invested each year.

One situation where this might not apply is if you are saving money for a down payment on a home. In that case, you may not want to have more than $35,000 in your RRSP because the maximum allowable withdrawal under the Home Buyers Plan for a first-time home buyer is only $35,000. Any amount you remove above $35,000 will be included in your income in the year of withdrawal. In addition, if you are saving money for other expenses, such as purchasing a car or if you are saving a rainy-day fund which you anticipate you will need in the near future, then the RRSP will not be the best option due to withdrawals being taxable. In those cases, you are better off parking the money in a TFSA where you can withdraw it tax free.

But, in theory, generally speaking, you should always try to maximize your RRSP and TFSA before having other investments for which you are earning income and paying taxes on.

What's more, with both the TFSA and RRSP, you never lose your contribution room. If you are unable to contribute in a certain year, that year's contribution room is carried forward forever.

The bottom line is if you do not have an RRSP or TFSA yet, and you are able to start saving money, you must seriously consider opening up one or both of these.

You can open a TFSA once you turn 18 or 19 years old, depending on the province you live in.

TIP #19 — *Always Double Check before Contributing and Other Important Points*

I have seen so many situations in which people have over-contributed to their RRSP or TFSA and have incurred ridiculous penalties. Thankfully it is possible to request the penalties be removed.

To avoid these over-contribution penalties in the first place, I strongly urge and recommend you always double check and triple check your contribution room. You can do this yourself by calling CRA, looking on your CRA "My Account" online or by looking at your Notice of Assessment, which should show your contribution room for both your RRSP and TFSA.

Also, never ever listen to the advice of people who work at the banks regarding the TFSA account. I have seen, way too many times, people over-contributing to their TFSAs because someone at their bank told them it was okay to contribute.

If you are not a resident of Canada for a certain year, then you lose that contribution room for that year.

If you are an American citizen living in Canada, you must speak to a United States accountant who is well versed in cross-border tax to obtain the correct advice regarding TFSAs (and everything else).

If you take out money from your TFSA, and you have already maxed out your contribution room, you must wait until January 1st of the following year to put that money back in.

You are allowed to take out money from your RRSP but it will be included in your income for that year and, therefore, depending on your level of income for that year, you may end up paying tax on that withdrawal.

The only way you can take money out of your RRSP without the withdrawal being included in your income is if you take out the money under the Home Buyers' Plan as a first-time home buyer or under the Lifelong Learning Plan to attend some sort of post-secondary education.

TIP #20 — *Be Wary of High-Fee Mutual Funds and Other Products*

People always ask me what they should invest in within their RRSP or TFSA. I do not give investment advice; I only explain the tax consequences of different types of investments. In the RESP, RRSP and TFSA, you can invest in GICs, savings bonds, high-interest savings accounts, publicly traded stocks, bonds, mutual funds, ETFs (Exchange Traded Funds) and some other types of investments.

I get very grumpy when I see people paying very high fees by owning certain types of mutual funds or listening to their bank advisor who earns a commission for selling their own bank's products. If you already have your money invested, whether in an RRSP, TFSA, RESP or any other account, find out exactly what fees you are paying on each investment you hold or on the account in general.

There are ways of paying much lower fees today, such as owning specific types of ETFs that are indexed to the market or specific sectors or even doing your own self-directed trading. For more information, I have listed some great resources in the Resources section at the back of this book.

Chapter 15

The Hardship of Being a
Self-Employed Tax Collector

Jerry gained tremendous experience over the years in his job as an architect. After many years of working for the same company, Jerry felt he needed a change. He yearned for more freedom and flexibility in his schedule and thought he could make more money by being self-employed. He decided to start his own small architectural consulting practice and work for himself.

He started to pick up some clients and he became pretty busy. He completely forgot to contact George and ask him for advice before venturing out on his own. He had a strange intuition that there must be tax consequences of being self-employed so he called George to find out if he needed to know any important information.

George said, "Congratulations on starting your own business, Jerry. You are joining 2.9 million other Canadians who are self-employed.[60]

"You must beware though, in Canada, running a business, or being self-employed, involves many rules, regulations, tax payments and tax filings. That is why a whole industry of accountants, lawyers, bookkeepers and other advisors exists to help you and others like you comply with government regulations and CRA tax obligations.

"I should warn you, most of my clients are small-business owners and I have become incredibly frustrated with how annoying, time consuming and costly it can be for small-business owners to comply with the tax system. You would think that the government and the CRA should make it as easy and seamless as possible to comply with tax filing and tax payment obligations. But alas, that is not the case. Let me explain. Let's start right at the beginning.

"Jerry, have you registered for GST yet?"[61]

"What are you talking about?"

George sighed and said, "Jerry, anyone who runs their own small business in Canada must become a tax collector and collect the Goods and Services Tax (GST) for the government as soon as they earn more than $30,000 of revenue in a year or in four consecutive quarters. There is an exception for some types of goods and services that are exempt or zero-rated, but for the most part, most businesses are required to go through this.

"You will need to register for a GST number, collect GST from your customers, ensure that you file your GST returns on time and pay your GST payable on time as well. You might find this to be quite a headache."

"Uh oh. I already earned more than $30,000 of revenue in the past few months after starting up. I didn't realize that I had to charge sales tax."

George said, "Why, Jerry? Why? Why do you make my life so difficult? We will now need to backdate the GST registration to the date on which you reached $30,000 of revenue.

"By the way, I find it really unfair that the government forces self-employed people to become tax collectors. If the government wants to collect a tax, it should find a more efficient way to do so without burdening every single self-employed individual, even those with only $30,000 of revenue.

"I can tell you from experience that the GST is a huge headache for the self-employed for many reasons.

"First, the government does not offer any compensation for this tax collecting service you are providing for them. Technically, you are able to deduct any GST you have paid on expenses from the amount of GST that you have to pay but that is meagre compensation for having to comply with this very complicated bureaucracy.

"Second, if you are even just one day late filing a GST return, a penalty of 5% of the amount owing will be charged. This is unfair and punitive. If they want to charge a late filing penalty, it should be a flat amount, not based on the amount of GST owing, which can be unfairly high.

"Third, if you do not pay your GST installments on time throughout the year, the CRA charges interest and penalties. If you owe $3,000 or more of GST in a certain year, then the following year, you must pay the GST/HST in quarterly installments.

"Fourth, if you provide services to another business, you must charge them GST. However, that business will claim the GST back on their GST return as an expense to reduce the GST that they owe to the government. To me, it makes no sense for businesses to have to charge other businesses GST, because each business claims back GST that they've paid on their expenses. Only the end-user, the non-business individual taxpayer who is purchasing the good or service, winds up paying GST. But the CRA still forces businesses to charge other businesses GST. It makes no logical sense; it creates a huge burden for businesses, especially small businesses, and provides no extra revenue to the government.

"Finally, when self-employed people collect GST from their customers, the money enters their bank account. Many self-employed people have a hard time collecting their bills and sometimes have to wait one, two, three or even more months to collect their bills. Therefore, when any money comes into their bank account, they are usually short on cash and need this cash to fund either business expenses or personal expenses.

"Jerry, hopefully you will not experience this but I am willing to bet that every single self-employed person and small-business owner will tell you that cash flow has been tight at least at some point, if not at many points, in their lives. I have to remind my clients all the time not to use the GST money. I always recommend they open a separate savings account and transfer all the GST collected into that separate account to keep it aside to be able to pay the CRA.

"In reality, it is very hard for self-employed people to manage their cash flow. The bureaucrats, academics and politicians responsible for creating the GST regime simply do not understand this and cannot sympathize with the situation. It is a huge burden on the hard-working, self-employed individual to keep track of the GST separately and ensure they don't spend it once it enters their bank account. Self-employed people are often married and have a family and children to support and many live pay cheque to pay cheque and have serious cash flow issues."

Jerry, with a worried look on his face, interrupted, "George, this sounds really difficult. I'm really scared; you are freaking me out. Please tell me you are going to help me make sure I file my GST returns and pay the GST on time!"

"Yes, Jerry, don't worry, that's what I'm here for. I strongly urge you to open a separate savings account and every time you collect a bill from a customer, you set aside the GST portion of that bill into that savings account. So many of my clients have not followed this advice and it has caused huge headaches for them."

Jerry took note of that critical piece of advice.

George continued, "Jerry, the worst aspect of the GST is that you will be obligated to pay it even if you have not collected the amount from your customer."

"George, what on earth do you mean? If I haven't collected the bill from my customer, how in the world am I supposed to pay the GST that has not been collected to the government?"

"Let me explain. Imagine it's December and you finish providing a report to one of your clients. You send them the report, they thank you and then you send them the bill. You must report the GST amount on that bill in your GST return for that calendar year even though you might not receive the actual payment for that bill until January or later.

"How can you possibly pay GST that you have not yet physically collected? It makes no sense and is very unfair for self-employed people that they are expected to pay out sales taxes they are collecting on behalf of the government before they have physically collected it.

"But, Jerry, you must abide by this system."

Jerry shook his head and almost started crying.

George, without any mercy, continued, "This is a great example of bureaucrats enacting legislation without thinking through all the unintended consequences.

"When you were an employee all those years, your T4 slip showed the amount of income you received during the year. Only income you received during the year was included in your tax return and you only paid tax on income you received.

"Welcome to the world of self-employment. You are now taxed on income and pay GST on imaginary future money. This is known as GST 'collectible' as opposed to 'collected.' Only government bureaucrats could come up with such incredulous Orwellian nonsense."

Jerry couldn't believe it. He agreed with George that it did not seem to make any sense but he realized he did not have a choice but to comply.

To Jerry's chagrin, George continued, "Another problem with the GST system for small-business owners is that the government frequently audits the claims that GST registrants make for any GST that they claim on their expenses. It is reasonable and understandable that the CRA must audit these claims and taxpayers must keep their receipts to prove the expenses were actually paid."

"George, I don't understand, what are you talking about? GST audits? What does that mean?"

"Jerry, when you file your GST return, you show your total sales and total GST that you collected on those sales. Then you are allowed to deduct GST 'input tax credits,' to reflect any GST that you pay on your business expenses. This reduces the amount of GST you have to pay out to the government.

"But the system is very burdensome and creates a lot of headaches for taxpayers and their accountants. The reason for this is because the CRA sometimes audits the claims people make on their GST returns. If someone claims a GST refund because they paid out more GST than they collected, the CRA might audit the return. Trust me; it is not fun dealing with these audits.

"I remember one of my clients once received a letter from the CRA in mid-February informing them that their GST return would be audited. The client sent me the letter and asked me to deal with it. I called the CRA auditor to tell him I would start the work but I requested more time as March and April were the height of tax season and I was very busy.

"The CRA auditor was not sympathetic and said the information must be provided to him within 30 days or less. I thought this was a totally unreasonable amount of time for the amount of work involved considering it was every accountant's busy season. Also, it's totally unreasonable considering that the CRA frequently takes months, sometimes even years, to respond to requests for adjustments, appeals and objections by taxpayers.

"The time, effort and cost involved in conducting these audits from the perspective of the CRA and from the perspective of the accountants and advisors are ridiculous, insane and unnecessary."

Jerry said, "Wow! That seems really frustrating. I'm sure you have other crazy stories to tell me about how insane the GST system is?"

George of course had more stories. He said, "Yes I do. I once had a client who came to me after receiving some flabbergasting letters from the CRA's GST department. Long story short, this guy had registered a GST account many years ago. He started to earn some commission income but it was always under $30,000 every year so he never collected any GST. He made a colossal mistake. The CRA came after him for all the GST each year. He misunderstood something fundamental about the GST regime.

"As soon as you register for a GST account you must start collecting GST on every dollar of income you earn, even if it will be under $30,000 every year. He thought that since his revenue was always under $30,000 he would be exempt as a small supplier. Oh boy, he thought wrong. What he should have done was closed the GST account as soon as he realized his revenue would always be under $30,000.

"At the end of the day, he was forced to pay out to the CRA more than $8,000 of GST that he never collected. It was a horrible outcome and a slap in the face to a hard-working, honest, well-meaning, low-income taxpayer. But that's what happens when Canadians complacently allow their government to enact complicated laws that the average human cannot understand."

Jerry couldn't believe it. "George, that is crazy! It seems like a really punitive and unfair system. I'm so happy I set up this meeting with you now. Do you think it's worth it for me to continue being self-employed? Maybe I should go back to my old job. It would be so much easier."

George chuckled, "Don't give up! I am here for you and if you follow my advice you will be okay. For now, let's register your GST account with the CRA."

George tried to register the GST account but they hit a snag. Jerry wanted to backdate the GST registration to six months prior, when he actually started his business activity. The CRA representative on the phone said, "If you want to back date the registration more than 30 days, you must send a special request to the Tax Centre, including proof that you were operating your business during that time, such as invoices from your sales." George explained to Jerry that this request can take months and months for the CRA to process.

Jerry was nervous. "How will I send out invoices to my clients in the meantime? Don't I need a GST number in order to charge GST?"

"Include the GST on your invoices and explain to your customers you will re-issue the invoices once you have the GST number."

"George, this is such a headache! Please tell me you have some ideas on how to make the GST system easier for self-employed people?"

George, with a big smile on his face, said, "Of course I do! First of all, there already exists the Quick Method for calculating GST. Some types of self-employed people and small-business owners are eligible for this. I would actually recommend this for you. It means that you collect the same amount of GST as you normally would but your GST return is simpler because instead of claiming the GST you paid out on your expenses, you simply remit a lower amount of GST to the CRA than you actually collected. So that will help you and will be worth it for you. This method is beneficial for people who don't have a lot of expenses.

"The main change the government needs to make for self-employed people is to increase the small supplier exemption limit. Currently, the limit is $30,000. So if your revenue is always under $30,000 every year, then you are exempt from registering for and from collecting GST. That number is way too low. The $30,000 limit has not been raised even once since the GST was first created in 1991! It should have increased every year with inflation but it has not, for some inexplicable reason.

"The government should immediately raise the limit to perhaps $100,000 of revenue and it should continue to increase the limit every year based on rates of inflation. We should not burden every self-employed individual who earns a penny more than $30,000 with the heavy bureaucracy and compliance costs that is the GST regime. We must raise this small supplier limit immediately to provide relief to self-employed people and small-business owners.

"This would really save a lot of money and time for small-business owners. If someone is earning $30,000 a year in revenue, they don't necessarily have enough funds to spend on an accountant every year and they also most likely don't have the time or know-how to deal with the burden of GST filing on their own. They have enough issues and difficulties managing their cash flow that they should not have to worry about collecting GST.

"The current limit of $30,000 encourages more people to enter the underground economy and conduct cash transactions to avoid having to deal with and worry about the GST.

"Currently, the 'small business deduction,' which is the low tax rate for small-business corporations, applies to net income up to $500,000. So why, when it comes to GST, does the government consider the definition of small business to be based on revenue of $30,000? Does that mean as soon as you earn more than $30,000 of revenue, you are now a medium- or large-sized business? Preposterous!

"It would be a huge help to small-business owners and self-employed individuals across the country to finally relieve them of this unnecessary, unfair and costly burden of being a tax collector for the government as it relates to GST.

"A self-employed individual has enough to worry about. Not only do they still have all their family obligations, they have incredibly stressful and busy lives as it comes to running their small business. This is what politicians and those who create these insane tax regimes do not understand. A small-business owner wears many hats. They have to manage their employees, manage their suppliers and payables, manage their customers and receivables, worry about marketing and advertising, worry about their competition, worry about their cash flow, worry about managing their expenses, worry about growing their business and, on top of all that, they have to worry about complying with the CRA on so many different fronts.

"There are payroll taxes, corporate taxes, GST/HST, personal taxes, along with other provincial regimes. There are too many different tax accounts and tax departments and tax filings for the self-employed and small-business owner to worry about.

"Also, many business owners in Canada complain about the amount of bureaucracy required to do business across different provinces. Each province has different sales tax rates and different sales tax authorities that you may need to register with. Some of my clients have complained to me that they actually find it easier to sell to customers in the United States than into different provinces within Canada.

"For example, New Brunswick, Newfoundland and Labrador, Nova Scotia and Prince Edward Island all have the Harmonized Sales Tax (HST) at 15%. Ontario has HST at 13%. HST is the federal GST and the provincial sales tax combined. Alberta, Nunavut, Northwest Territories and Yukon only have the federal 5% GST. All the other provinces have GST at 5% along with their provincial sales taxes. British Columbia and Manitoba have a 7% provincial sales tax, Saskatchewan has a 6% sales tax and Quebec has the QST at 9.975%.[62] Are you confused yet? In British Columbia, Manitoba, Saskatchewan and Quebec, you might have to register with their provincial sales tax authority if you conduct business in their province. So in addition to filing your GST return to the CRA, you will have to file a provincial sales tax return to those provinces.

"Exempting self-employed people from GST obligations will go a long way to helping them out, making things simpler and easier for them in terms of both their cash flow, their costs of complying with tax law and having one less thing to worry about.

"Also, GST returns should be reported and filed on a cash basis. GST should only be paid to the government after it is actually collected from the customer. No one should have to remit taxes to the government that they never actually collected. This would also help self-employed people with their cash flow.

"Last, the GST return for a self-employed sole proprietor should simply be included within the personal tax return filing. The obligation to file a separate GST return increases the possibility of incurring penalties for filing the return late. Why does the self-employed individual have to file a separate GST return? There's really no good rationale for it. It can very easily and simply be combined as a couple of line items within the T2125 Statement of Business Activities that the self-employed individual must already file as part of his or her personal tax return.

"Also, the GST that must be paid should be combined with the personal income tax as one payment. This type of streamlining would help self-employed individuals save a lot of hassle. It would mean less chance for penalties and interest on late payments since there would be fewer physical tax payments to make.

"Think about it. The individual tax returns that we file include both federal income tax and provincial income tax in one tax return. The CRA receives the provincial tax return and the actual provincial income tax and then works it out within their system and allocates the information and money back to each province (with the exception of Quebec). So if the CRA can coordinate with the provinces, then surely it can coordinate within its own agency in administrating both income tax and GST within one combined filing."

Jerry said, "That all sounds amazing, George. You have my vote. Maybe you should write a book with all your proposals one day?"

"Maybe I will Jerry, maybe I will."

"I don't think I can handle any more for today. Thanks for everything, as always."

Jerry returned to his home office where he continued to grow his successful consulting practice while George returned to his frustrating work, grumpy as always.

TIP #21 — *Set Up GST Properly at the Start*

My most important piece of advice is to always set aside the GST you collect. I cannot stress the importance of this enough. Remember, you are a tax collector. Every time you collect a bill with GST (or HST or any other provincial sales tax), you must always take that GST/HST and set it aside, never touch it, never spend it, never look at it, never fantasize about it. It is not your money. It belongs to the government! So, keep it aside so you can pay it to them by the correct due date.

Here are some other important tips for GST/HST.

Some goods and services are exempt from GST/HST and some are zero-rated so make sure you know if you are obligated to register for GST/HST and what category your business falls under. I have provided links to the Guide for GST/HST on the Resources pages.

Remember if your revenue will never hit $30,000 in a year or four consecutive fiscal quarters, then you do not need to register for the GST/HST.

Once you register, you must collect GST/HST on every dollar of revenue, even if your revenue is under $30,000.

If you have very few expenses, then the Quick Method might be more beneficial for you. I have included information on the Quick Method in the Resources section as well.

Different provinces have different sales tax rates and different regimes. For example, New Brunswick, Newfoundland, Nova Scotia, Ontario and Prince Edward Island are all under HST, so you only need to register HST directly with the CRA. Alberta, Northwest Territories, Nunavut and Yukon only have the GST so you only need to register for GST directly with the CRA. In British Columbia, Saskatchewan, Manitoba and Quebec, you may also need to register with that province's tax authority in addition to the CRA.

My dream is that Canadians could become self-employed without being required to become tax collectors for the government. Until that dream comes true, you must comply with the above GST/HST requirements.

TIP #22—Bookkeeping Essentials

When you are self-employed, you must become a bookkeeper. You must keep track of all your revenue and sales taxes collected. You must keep track of each expense, according to its proper category, and keep every receipt for every expense.

This can be a daunting task but it is absolutely imperative that you ensure your bookkeeping is up to date throughout the year to avoid a messy, costly, stressful tax filing experience at year-end.

You can hire a bookkeeper to take care of this task for you or you can try doing it yourself. I have listed some great book-keeping tools on the Resources pages. Many of these tools allow you to scan in receipts using an app on your phone, they upload bank and credit card transactions automatically in their cloud-based systems, allowing you to do invoicing and keep track of your receivables all in one seamless system, which you can access online from anywhere in the world. I highly recommend using one of those systems instead of putting all your receipts into a shoe box and then bringing it to your accountant at the end of the year.

When you file your tax return for the year, you must report all your business income and expenses on the "T2125 Statement of Business or Professional Activities" form. The link to this form is included in the Resources section at the back of the book. This statement is not as complicated as it seems. It simply lists your revenue and all your expenses. It also shows how the deductions work for car expenses, home office, depreciation and more.

As with every aspect of Canadian tax, you need to be proactive, prudent, stay on top of things from day one and seek help when you need it.

Chapter 16

One Equals Two—Double CPP

Jerry's business was doing well. It grew faster than he expected and he was enjoying the work immensely. He followed George's sage advice and made sure to set aside all the GST he collected in a separate bank account and he never touched it.

The first year of running the business passed and it came time to prepare Jerry's tax return. Jerry could not believe how much work it was to keep track of all his business expenses. He called George to confirm that it was really necessary to retain every single receipt for every expense and keep track of every expense in their appropriate categories. George insisted that it was, in fact, necessary.

"Jerry, I wish self-employed people did not have to keep track of expenses or hang onto receipts but the T2125 Statement of Business Activities forces you to show all your expenses by category so CRA can determine if they are reasonable or not. If they seem unreasonable, the CRA may audit the expenses and then you would have to send in every single receipt to the CRA so they could verify that your business expenses are accurately reported.

"This whole system is very costly in terms of your time, effort, hassle, not to mention bookkeeping and accounting fees. It is also expensive for the CRA (read: the taxpayer!), which has to employ auditors to conduct audits of hard-working, busy, self-employed people."

Jerry sighed, "If only there were a better way."

"Of course there is a better way. How about this?

"Allow the self-employed to report total revenue without any expenses. No need to keep track of expenses by category, no need to keep receipts, no need for CRA audits ever again!"

"But George, that would be extremely unfair. We need to deduct our valid business expenses from our revenue in order to pay a reasonable amount of tax on our actual profit. If I earn $10,000 of revenue but have business expenses of $5,000, I shouldn't have to pay tax on $10,000 of revenue. I should pay tax on the $5,000 of profit."

"Jerry, you are wise. I'm impressed with how knowledgeable you are now. But you didn't let me finish. All we need to do is tax the revenue from the business at a lower rate. It's very simple. Effectively the taxes paid would be similar, but we skip all the costs and bureaucracy associated with the current system."

"This sounds similar to your plan of abolishing all tax credits and deductions and simply lowering the rate of tax to make up for it."

"Exactly! For self-employed people, why not give them a choice? Option A and Option B. Option A would be revenue. Option B would be net income after expenses. So, if someone feels they have a lot of expenses, then they can file their tax return with all the expenses, by category, and risk a CRA audit and keep all their receipts. But at least it's their choice.

"If someone feels they would rather not have to keep any receipts and not have to maintain immaculate books and records for all their expenses, then let them pay tax based on their revenue instead of their profit."

Jerry liked this idea. Giving the taxpayer more choice and the potential to reduce bureaucracy was very appealing to him. In the meantime, he knew he still had to comply with the current system in place. So he sent George all of his information.

George prepared the tax returns and called Jerry, "Jerry, congratulations on making so much money from your business. I'm very happy for you. Oh, and by the way, you owe tax of $20,800."

Jerry said, "Excuse me?"

George suggested that Jerry come into his office so he could explain his tax return to him.

"Jerry, you made a lot of money so obviously you have to pay tax. Your revenue was $100,000 and you had $25,000 of expenses, so your net income from the business was $75,000. Your taxes payable on $75,000 of income is $15,000."[63]

Jerry said, "Okay fine, I'll pay it. I have the money saved up. But on the phone, you said my tax bill was $20,800. Now you're saying it's $15,000. Which one is it?"

"Jerry, do you remember, back when you were an employee, all those deductions from your pay cheque?"

"Yes of course. I remember CPP, EI and income tax deductions."

"Well, now that you are self-employed you are exempt from EI but you still have to pay income tax, so that's the $15,000. The other $5,800 is CPP.[64] So $15,000 + $5,800 = $20,800."

Jerry said, "Wait a minute. $5,800 of CPP? Are you sure? It seems high. I remember when I used to work, my T4 slip only showed something like $2,900 of CPP. Are you sure you didn't make a mistake?"

"Jerry, do I ever make mistakes? It's true that you only paid $2,900 from your pay and that's what shows up on your T4. But do not forget your employer also pays CPP out of their own pocket. They must match your contribution so they were paying the same amount of CPP you were paying."

"So how does this affect me now that I'm self-employed. I don't have any employees so why should I care about this?"

George said, "You are wrong! You do have an employee!"

"George, I think I would know if I have an employee. Trust me, I am doing all the work myself. I have zero employees."

"Not so fast Jerry. You are self-employed. You are the employee! You are employing yourself. You are an employer and an employee at the same time and therefore you must actually pay double the amount of Canada

Pension Plan contributions that you were before. That's why you now owe $5,800 of CPP."

"I have to pay double? I am my own employer? That seems a bit crazy. But hey, at least when I retire and receive my pension from CPP, I will get double the amount back, right?"

George laughed, "Are you crazy? Do you think you live in a country where the tax system makes sense? You will still receive the same pension as everyone else even though you are paying double the contribution into it. That's the price of being self-employed."

"Hmm. So let me get this straight. The government of Canada considers me to be two people even though I am one person?"

"Well, not in the literal sense."

"But when I retire and collect my pension from the Canada Pension Plan, I don't get the pension of two people?"

"Correct!"

Jerry said, "I give up. I will do as you say and I will stop questioning, I just don't have the energy!"

"To be fair, there is some logic behind this. The government believes $5,800 is required in contributions for each pensioner. That $5,800 is split between the employee and the employer. You happen to be both the employee and employer so you must pay the whole cost.

"Jerry, if you want to avoid paying into CPP, you would need to incorporate, run your business through the corporation and then the corporation can pay you a dividend instead of a salary, thus avoiding CPP. We can discuss that another time if you'd like.

"Before I forget, I must tell you after you pay the $20,800 of income tax and CPP for this year, along with the GST that you owe, you need to start saving money for next year's taxes also."

"What are you talking about? Why would you bring up next year's taxes? This year's taxes are bad enough."

George said, "You will have to pay in installments for next year for both your personal tax and the GST. Remember, you are self-employed. You are responsible to pay for your own taxes and the CRA does not want to wait until the end of the year to receive your money. You will need to pay the tax throughout the year.

"Keep setting aside all the GST you collect in that separate bank account of yours. Also, add in 15-20% of all your other revenue as well just to be safe to cover the income tax and CPP.

"I also highly recommend you set up 'My Business Account' online at the CRA website for your GST account to make it easier to track your payments and filings."

Jerry grudgingly accepted George's advice. He paid all his taxes owing and began saving for next year's taxes. He went home that night and he told Elaine everything that happened. She laughed and was thankful she was still working as an employee and didn't have to deal with this complicated bureaucracy.

TIP #23 — *Save for Tax Installments*

If you are self-employed, you will most likely owe tax at the end of the year when you file your tax return.

As I recommended previously with GST/HST, you must try your best to set aside money from all your revenue that comes in to have cash on hand to pay the taxes at year-end or pay in installments throughout the year.

If you owed $3,000 or more of tax in a certain year, then the next year, you must pay installments throughout the year instead of waiting until the following April 30th to pay your taxes owing.

Therefore, please remember, I beg you, to set aside a portion of your revenue.

To estimate how much revenue to save, a good rule of thumb is simply to set aside all the GST/HST that you collect.

Then, to calculate how much income tax and CPP you owe, simply estimate two numbers—your total revenue for the year and your total expenses.

Revenue minus expenses equals net income.

Take that net income figure, put it into one of the tax calculators I suggest in the Resources pages. You will then see your income taxes payable.

You will also owe CPP. This can be calculated as your net income from the business minus $3,500 multiplied by 10.5%. So, for example, if your net income is $50,000, it would be $50,000−$3,500 = $46,500 x 10.5% = $4,882.50.

Once you earn $58,700 of self-employment income then you hit the maximum amount that you need to pay into CPP. So when you do your calculation, if you are above $58,700 of self-employment income, then you know the exact amount of CPP you need to pay, which is the maximum for the year, $5,796. The above information is based on the 2020 rates for CPP. Check the Resources pages for links on CPP rates. These rates can change every year.

Remember to set up "My Business Account" online for your GST/HST account. The link to this can be found in the Resources section.

Sorry this isn't easy. I wish it was!

Chapter 17

ARE CORPORATIONS EVIL LEGAL FICTIONS?

As time passed, Jerry and Elaine's children grew up and attended their local high school. Elaine was working full time as a writer and she took pleasure in her work. Jerry's business expanded significantly. He was enjoying growing his business but he couldn't believe how much tax he was paying. Jerry met a lot of other small-business owners at networking events. Most of them ran their businesses through corporations.

Jerry thought maybe he could benefit from one of these corporations so he set up a meeting with George to discuss the idea of opening a corporation.

George was excited to hear how Jerry's business was growing. "Jerry, it is truly amazing your business has grown so much. By the way, did you hear about that couple from Vancouver Island, British Columbia?"

"I've heard B.C. is beautiful but I've never visited and no I didn't hear about that couple. Please enlighten me."

"Okay, Jerry, but brace yourself for this one. A couple from Vancouver Island was awarded nearly $1.7 million in damages after a judge criticized the CRA for the ruination of their business and personal lives by 'high-handed, reprehensible and malicious actions.'[65] This couple was victimized by CRA auditors who alleged tax evasion at the couple's restaurant and other businesses. The couple was charged with 21 counts of tax evasion for taking out $1.7 million from their business. They were acquitted of all charges by a judge who said the CRA used 'voodoo accounting' to support its case. The couple sued for malicious prosecution, alleging that the CRA auditor and senior investigator targeted them without any evidence of wrongdoing.

"The judge wrote that 'the CRA used the powers of the state in the form of a criminal prosecution to wrongfully and maliciously prosecute.' The judge noted that the CRA investigators suppressed and misstated evidence and discussed 'the unfortunate culture' within the CRA. It was found the CRA auditors in the department were e-mailing each other saying such things as, 'after 85 charges, doesn't a guilty verdict call for a guillotine?' and 'I can't wait to read the edition after the guilty verdict' referring to a front-page newspaper story. The judge wrote that 'CRA employees looked forward with unprofessional glee to the plaintiffs' anticipated conviction and sentencing and their resulting ruination.' The judge stated that the CRA and this particular investigator 'do not acknowledge their wrongdoing or violation of their professional standards. They expressed no apology and were without remorse. Given the opportunity they would pursue the plaintiffs again on the same basis.'"

Jerry was floored. "George, is this some kind of warning you are trying to provide me? Are you saying I should not open a corporation and should not continue expanding my business?"

"No, Jerry, don't worry. I will ensure your books are clean and tax returns filed on time, don't worry at all. There might be some advantages for you if you run your business through a corporation, at least in the long run. But there are also some disadvantages which, of course, include a whole bunch of increased bureaucracy."

"Well, no surprise there. Please tell me everything I need to know."

George obliged. "If you open up a corporation then this corporation is considered a separate legal entity from you and the corporation must file its own tax return."

Jerry interjected, "Another tax return? You can't be serious?"

"Yes, another tax return."

"So are you saying, in addition to my individual tax return and my GST return, I will have another tax return—the corporate tax return?"

"Yes, exactly, the corporate tax return, or T2. Isn't this fun?"

"Why would I go to all this trouble? Are you sure it's worth it?"

"Well, from a purely tax perspective, it's only worth it if you earn enough profit in the corporation such that you won't need all of it for personal use. This will result in a nice, big, juicy tax deferral."

"George, I don't understand. Can you speak in English please? What is a tax deferral?"

"Okay, Jerry, stay with me. Let's look at your tax return from last year. Your profit from the business was $75,000. You paid $15,000 of income tax, which is 20%.

"Let's now imagine you earned this profit in your corporation. The tax rate on the first $500,000 of profit in the corporation is only 12.2%.[66] This is a nice low rate due to the small business deduction available to small business owners. Imagine you didn't need to take any money from this profit for your own personal salary or personal use. The tax on the $75,000, at a rate of 12.2%, would be $9,150. Personal tax on this amount was $15,000, whereas within the corporation the tax is $9,150, resulting in tax savings of almost $6,000.

"Let's imagine another case in which you had other personal income pushing you into the highest tax bracket, which is 53.53%.[67] On an extra $75,000 of profit, you would pay personal tax of $40,000. However by leaving this profit in the corporation and having it taxed at only 12.2%, you are saving almost $31,000 in taxes."

"Wow, George, that's amazing. Why wouldn't everyone incorporate their business? The corporate tax rate is so much lower than the high personal tax rates."

"Well, remember Jerry, not every business owner earns enough leftover profit to take advantage of the low small business corporate tax rate.

"Oh, and don't forget about my fee. I charge a lot more to file your corporate tax return every year. There is a lot more work involved, unfortunately.

"Also, many people incorporate their businesses to keep their business separate from their personal assets and personal funds in order to decrease their liability should they ever be sued. So most business owners, as they grow, are encouraged to incorporate their businesses instead of operating as a self-employed individual."

Jerry said, "My business keeps growing, I want to hire people soon and I want to keep the business completely separate from my personal affairs so let's do this."

"Okay, first things first. Jerry, we must first decide whether to open an Ontario corporation or a federal corporation. If you open an Ontario corporation, your corporation must file an annual information return to the Ministry of Finance of Ontario. Thankfully, this one-page form is already included in the annual corporate tax return that has to be filed each year to the CRA. The CRA and Ministry of Finance of Ontario have coordinated such that you don't have to file a separate provincial tax return. It's easy, simple and clean. I love it!"

"George, I can't believe I just heard you say the words 'I love it' regarding the tax system."

"Yes, for once, they got it right. But let's not jump the gun. For some inexplicable reason, if someone has a federally incorporated corporation, they must file a totally separate annual information return to Industry Canada. This one-page silly form is not included in the T2 corporate tax return.

"Industry Canada charges $20 to each corporation to file this annual return. It can be filed online, only takes a couple of minutes and is very easy to file. However, what I fail to understand is why can't this form be included in the T2 corporate tax return to make things easier for the small-business owner?

"Jerry, the following story actually happened to a client of mine. It drove me bananas.

"I e-filed the client's corporate tax return to the CRA and all was hunky dory. This was a very busy individual with a family to take care of and a small business to run. You know how it is with people receiving a million e-mails every day. He never noticed the e-mail reminder from Industry Canada requesting him to file the annual information return for his corporation.

"Since he ended up being in default of that filing, Industry Canada dissolved his corporation. He was required to file a form and pay a $200 fee to re-open or 'revive' the corporation. I thought this was absolute insanity.

"First, Industry Canada should be able to coordinate with the CRA to include the annual return within the corporate tax return, the same way every province does. This annual information return only requests the name and address of the corporation and the director's information to keep it updated on their file.

"If the CRA can coordinate with every province's Ministry of Finance to include this form within the T2 to spare the small-business owner from worrying about yet another filing, why can't the CRA coordinate with Industry Canada?

"I e-mailed my Member of Parliament, the Minister of Revenue and the Minister of Finance about this. I received a generic reply from one of them thanking me for my e-mail and I have yet to see any changes made to this insane lack of coordination between Industry Canada and the CRA.

"I spoke to someone at Industry Canada over the phone and explained my frustrations and all they said was the CRA and Industry Canada are two totally separate departments. I said 'Are you telling me the CRA can't coordinate with Industry Canada but they are able to coordinate with every provincial Ministry of Finance?'

"Second, why is there a need for a $20 annual filing fee? In my mind, this is a cash grab. If you want to open a corporation and run a small business, you have to pay to incorporate the corporation, then you have to pay a filing fee every year to keep it open and on top of all those silly fees, you have to pay corporate income tax every year.

"Last, the fact that Industry Canada dissolves these corporations when people don't file these returns is completely ridiculous, considering they charge an extra $200 fee to re-open the corporation. Honestly, it's bonkers."

"Hmm. I think I want to open an Ontario corporation."

George said, "Good call, Jerry. Unless you want to operate your business across Canada, then a federal corporation might be better but you may still have to register your corporation with every province anyways. Welcome to Canadian bureaucracy. Now, let's move on to the next order of business. You better take a deep breath because this one is a real gem."

Jerry took several deep breaths.

George frowned and said, "Since your business was started as a self-employed individual and now you want to run your business through a corporation, you will have to sell your existing assets from yourself to the corporation."

Jerry was extremely confused, "George, what are you talking about? Sell my assets from myself to my corporation? But I own my corporation! So I have to sell my assets to myself? George, have you lost your mind?"

"Somehow shockingly after many years of doing this job, I have not lost my mind. The politicians and bureaucrats who created all these insane rules have lost their minds but I have not. You will need to file a ridiculous, non-sensical, bureaucratic, unnecessary form. This is known as a 'Section 85 Rollover.' It is a form that allows you to sell the assets of the business that you own personally to the new corporation without paying capital gains tax."

"George, I have no assets. I am merely a simple architect who provides consulting services. There are no assets. I mean, I have a computer and a desk, and some paper, that's about it. So I think you really have lost your mind."

"Jerry, you know all those clients you have? You know how they keep referring new clients to you? You know how you have a great reputation and your brand name is respected and sought after?"

Jerry blushed.

"That is your asset. We accountants call it 'goodwill.' It refers to the value of your business, your name, your reputation and your list of customers. You are now selling all of this to the corporation."

Jerry shook his head and once again almost started to cry.

George continued, "Normally when one sells assets, a 'capital gain' must be recorded. A capital gain occurs when you sell assets for more than what you paid for them. Half of the capital gain is included in your income and you pay tax on it.

"However, in this case, since you are selling the assets to your own corporation, the government acknowledges that it would not be fair to charge capital gains tax when you are selling the assets to your own corporation. So they allow the assets to be sold at a value that is equal to their cost, so there is no capital gain, but in order to accomplish this feat a Section 85 Rollover form must be filed. Most taxpayers cannot do this complicated filing themselves and have to pay an accountant or lawyer or both to do this properly."

Jerry still seemed confused. He asked, "George, you're killing me. Isn't there a way to just record the value of the goodwill on the books of the corporation without all this crazy bureaucracy?"

"Well, there certainly should be. If someone starts a business as a self-employed person, like you did, and later on decides to incorporate, you should be able to record the assets on the books of the corporation without the need for these complicated filings.

"Of course, these complicated filings are good business for accountants and lawyers and for CRA auditors and CRA employees but it's a burden for everyone else.

"Jerry, don't worry; we will get that form filed. That's what I'm here for."

"Thanks, George. I know I can always count on you."

TIP #24 — *To Incorporate or Not to Incorporate*

One of the most common questions I am asked is whether a person should incorporate their small business. Everyone's situation is different so it's hard to give generic advice.

But generally speaking, if you are earning a level of net income (after expenses) such that you have way more money than you need for your personal living expenses, then incorporating could definitely be advantageous. This is because of the small business deduction available to the corporation. The net income, in the small-business corporation, is taxed at a much lower rate than the high rates of tax on personal income. You can leave your net income in the corporation, pay the corporate tax and have more after-tax money, within the corporation, to re-invest in the business, build up some cash reserves or make other investments.

Of course, remember that you will always pay personal tax as soon as you withdraw money from the corporation. But if you can leave extra money in the corporation, over the long term, you will save on tax and have more money to invest, until you withdraw the money from the corporation and incur personal tax.

If your income is going to be pretty low every year and you know you will need every penny of profit from your business for your own personal salary to fund your personal living expenses, then incorporation may not provide any tax advantage. It is wise to speak to a corporate lawyer in addition to an accountant before incorporating to determine the best structure.

Chapter 18

It's Not You; It's Me

Some time passed and Elaine decided it was time for a change. She and Jerry sat down for dinner and Elaine told him she wanted to do some major renovations on their house. Jerry agreed to this plan because he didn't have the energy to argue. They did some research and estimated the renovations would cost $50,000.

It seemed like a lot of money but Jerry's business was doing very well. He had amassed a nice chunk of change in his corporation so he decided to withdraw $50,000 from his corporation and transfer it to his personal bank account to pay for the renovations.

As another tax year was coming to a close, he met with George to begin the process of filing his corporate tax return. Jerry provided George with his balance sheet and income statement from the corporation. He was very proud of his bookkeeping skills.

George looked over everything very carefully. He noticed there was an expense on the income statement called "Salary" for $50,000. George asked Jerry what this was and Jerry explained it was the salary he paid to himself to fund the house renovations.

George shook his head. Jerry said, "What now! What did I do wrong?"

George took a deep breath and said, "Jerry, do you think you can just take out money from your corporation like that?"

"Why not? This is my corporation; it's my money. I know I have to show this as personal income on my tax return. I will show it as self-employment income like I did previously. After all, I am self-employed. You think I didn't know about this?"

George shook his head even more. His head sunk into his hands and he started crying.

"George, why are you crying? Please, calm down. I'm sorry! I didn't mean to hurt you. Tell me, what is going on?"

George lifted up his head and wiped the tears from his face. "Oh, Jerry. You cause me such grief. I have bad news for you. You are not self-employed."

"Yes, I am. I do not have an employer. I employ myself. Remember? I started my own business? George, you really are losing your mind. I am most definitely self-employed. You told me yourself I have to pay double the amount of CPP because I employ myself."

George with a frown on his face, said, "Sorry, Jerry, that's not how it works. You incorporated your small business. Remember, the corporation is separate from you.

"Therefore, you are an employee of your corporation and your corporation will need to open a payroll tax account with the CRA, deduct CPP and income tax from your salary, pay that tax to the CRA along with the employer portion of CPP, then pay your after-tax net salary to you, and provide you with a T4 slip at the end of the year."

Jerry was shocked to hear this. He said, "What are you talking about? Why do I have to go to all that trouble? I don't have any other employees! It's just me, myself and I. Can't I just take out the salary, show it on my personal tax return and I'll pay the personal tax and CPP when I file my personal tax return? Honestly, what's the big deal?"

"Listen, I agree with what you're saying. But alas, that is not how it works. Also, we need to do a calculation to see if it would be better to pay you a dividend rather than a salary. That might be more advantageous and a bit easier as well from a bureaucratic perspective, but that's a whole other conversation!

"This is why I get paid the big bucks.

"Nothing is simple, easy or logical when it comes to tax returns.

"Jerry, if you try what you are suggesting, you will be in big scary trouble. I strongly urge and recommend you do not show this $50,000 as self-employment income on your tax return.

"Let me tell you a story that happened to another client of mine. This client was just like you. She was very hard working and owned her own small business that she managed and ran by herself.

"She started a business from scratch, taking a risk, worked very hard and built up a nice growing business that employed other hard-working Canadians in an industry in which many larger corporations would outsource the work overseas for cheaper labour. How did the government reward her? By sending her on a two-year bureaucratic nightmare!

"Here is what happened. For two years, she was not aware of the complex rules regarding how to withdraw money from her own corporation as a salary. She did not know, that even though she owned her own corporation, she cannot withdraw money from the corporation as a salary without doing proper deductions for CPP and income tax and filing T4 slips.

"Instead, she did what you wanted to do, which would be the logical, simple and intuitive step of transferring the money to her personal account, recording it as a salary expense in the company books and recording the amount as personal income on her personal tax return. This was simple, intuitive and logical.

"On her personal tax return, she recorded the amount as self-employment income, which generated the exact correct amounts of CPP payable and income taxes payable, which she paid on time when she filed her personal tax accounts.

"What did the CRA do in this situation? A payroll audit was conducted to examine the corporation's books. The CRA auditor came to the taxpayer's place of business, sat her down and found out this is how she recorded her salary. She then plunged her down a rabbit hole that took two years to climb out of. In my opinion, it was totally unnecessary and insane.

"She had to go back in time for two years and prepare T4 slips for herself for each year but she also had to pay the payroll taxes from the corporation.

"For each year, the CRA sent assessments for CPP payable, both the employee and the employer portions, and the income taxes payable. The bill came to over $7,000! I was astounded. I begged the CRA not do this. I begged the CRA auditor to try to understand that these amounts of CPP and income tax were already paid. I begged the CRA auditor to look at my client's personal tax account so she could see clearly that the thousands of dollars of tax and CPP had already been paid to CRA.

"I asked the CRA auditor to explain how my client's corporation would be able to come up with the cash to make these payroll tax payments considering they'd already been paid to the CRA from the personal tax account. It made no sense! I asked to speak to a supervisor but nothing could be done to change their minds.

"The CRA said, to be fair, that they would of course reassess her personal tax account for those two years and then refund the CPP and income tax that was paid personally. I thought that this was pure bureaucratic nonsense. The CPP and income tax had been paid but through the wrong procedure. What an absolutely outrageous tax system whereby a small-business owner cannot even pay themselves from their business without worrying about excessive bureaucracy from the CRA.

"After the payroll taxes were assessed as owing from the corporation, the corporation received letters from the collections department at the CRA demanding that the taxpayer pay the amounts owing at once or face legal action. I explained to the collections officer the entire situation. The money is already at the CRA. Why don't you, on the CRA end, just take it from their personal tax accounts and transfer it over on your end? Why are you forcing the taxpayer to do this? This is a hard-working individual, who paid herself a salary of only $30,000 for each year. We aren't talking about a rich millionaire or billionaire! I was so frustrated and grumpy because of this that I filed a service complaint to explain everything that was happening.

"I filed a T1 adjustment on her personal tax account to claim back the refund of CPP and income taxes that were already paid so then the business owner could take those refunds, deposit them in their corporation and pay the payroll taxes owing from there. This process, from start to finish, literally took two years! It was two years of back and forth, of stress and of receiving threatening letters from the collections department.

"All this small-business owner ever wanted to do was pay herself a salary. She showed the income properly on her personal tax return and paid the exact correct amount of CPP and income tax. Her mistake was the timing, method and procedure of how she paid herself."

Jerry listened to the story intently. He said, "Okay George, I do not want that to happen to me. I will listen to you. You tell me exactly what I need to do to pay myself the salary correctly so I don't have to go through that nightmare!"

George explained everything to him. He opened the CRA payroll account, he calculated the CPP and income tax deductions on the salary, explained how Jerry could make the tax payment to CRA online and he ensured Jerry he would file the T4 slip on time every year.

"Jerry, I'm sorry you have to go through all of this. I really wish people like you, owners of small business corporations, could have a simpler time complying with the tax system. You really should be able to withdraw money from the corporation and record it as income on your personal tax return, without going through all this hassle of CRA payroll accounts, source deductions and T4 filings.

"The current system is quite absurd when you think about it. Your intuitive idea of how you originally wanted to withdraw the money was logical, rational and sensible, and would have saved a lot of time, cost and frustration for you as a small business owner."

Jerry agreed with George, as usual. He thought that everything he was required to do to pay himself from his own business was insane and went home that night pretty grumpy himself. Elaine detected the grumpiness. They were lying in bed talking. Elaine said, "Well, despite all this, at least our house is now beautifully renovated."

Jerry didn't reply to her and he proceeded to cry himself to sleep.

TIP #25 — *Plan Ahead*

Salaries, dividends, loans, oh my. Taking out money from your corporation can be complicated and you will need proper tax advice on an annual basis for this bureaucratic nightmare. The tax rates change every year and the rules can change every year and the strategies can change every year, so folks, don't try this at home! Be very careful.

If you decide to pay yourself with a salary, remember you must deduct CPP and income tax from your salary. You must pay the deductions, along with the employer portion of CPP, to the CRA by the 15th of the month for the previous month's payroll and file a T4 by the end of February for the previous year's salary.

Paying yourself a salary generates RRSP contribution room for yourself personally and the salary is a deductible expense on the corporate income statement so every dollar of salary you pay yourself reduces corporate income and therefore corporate tax. You pay the tax personally instead of within the corporation.

If you pay yourself a dividend, then you would file a T5, instead of a T4, and there would be no CPP or tax deductions. The dividend is not a deductible expense in the corporation and does not generate RRSP contribution for you personally but, at lower levels of personal income, a dividend generates lower personal income taxes than a salary due to the dividend tax credit. Overall, whether you pay yourself a salary or dividend, the total personal and corporate income tax, when added together, should be roughly the same.

There are pros and cons of each option so you need to consult with an advisor or accountant so they have a clear and full picture of your complete financial situation to determine the best option for you specifically.

For the love of God, make sure you stay on top of this and plan it every year *before* the year ends. If you know you need a fixed amount of money every year for your personal living expenses, then tell that to your accountant so this can be planned in advance, at the beginning of the year, instead of waiting until after the year-end, and after you've already withdrawn the money.

Chapter 19

PAYING TAX ON IMAGINARY INCOME

Jerry's business continued to grow. He rented a large amount of office space, hired some employees, bought quite a lot of furniture and computers to outfit the offices, and spent a nice amount of money doing some beautiful renovations to the office. He loved being the boss, sitting in his corner office, supervising what he had created from scratch. All was going well. That is until another year-end was approaching.

One day, as Jerry was going over the books for the year, he was agitated. He knew that every year, something comes up unexpected with regards to his tax returns. He was trying to determine what it would be this year. He looked over his income statement that he prepared for George. The income statement showed a loss of $10,000. He was upset that he lost money this year but he knew it was because of the investments he made into the business to get the office up and running. He also was smart enough to know that having a loss meant he wouldn't pay any tax for the year, which made him feel a bit better.

Jerry gathered all his year-end tax documents for the corporation and went to see George.

George looked over the income statement. He scrutinized every line of it and asked Jerry to see the full "general ledger" showing every single item that was claimed as an expense. Jerry was apprehensive. He knew he did something wrong; he couldn't bear the suspense any longer.

"George, lay it on me. Tell me why are you looking at my income statement in such thorough detail? I want to hear what you have to say right now, I can't wait any longer!"

"Jerry, I have some bad news for you."

Jerry's heart sank.

"You know how your income statement is showing a loss of $10,000?"

Jerry nodded his head as his eyes began to well up with tears.

"Well, congratulations! For tax purposes your profit is actually $20,000."

Jerry looked at George incredulously. "George, is this some kind of cruel joke? Are you sure you are an accountant? How is it possible I made $20,000 in profit? I spent so much money this year on renovations to the offices, and on new furniture and computers for my employees. If I add that altogether, I recall spending about $30,000. So what are you talking about?"

"Oh, Jerry, what am I ever going to do with you? Listen to me very carefully. All that money you spent on furniture, computers and renovations to the office is not really an expense."

"It's not an expense? What on earth are you talking about? Of course, it's an expense. I paid for it. Since I paid for it and it was for the business, I wrote it off."

"I know you paid for it. So it seems like an expense. But our lovely government thinks otherwise. You cannot write it off as an expense."

"Why not?"

"Jerry, do you even know what a write-off is?"

"No, I don't."

"Well, I do. And I'm the one who decides whether you can write it off. These are not write-offs as expenses, these are 'capital assets.'"

"Capital what now?"

George explained, "Capital assets. The furniture, computers and office renovations are expenses that provide you with a future benefit for many years to come. Your business will own these items, known as assets, for years and years and therefore you have to show them as capital assets on your balance sheet. You cannot show the full amount as an expense in your income statement in the year you purchased them."

"George, please, in what kind of a world would an expense not be an expense?"

"Well, every year, you can record an expense to reflect the value of these assets going down over time. We call this 'depreciation' or 'amortization.' So, every year, you will be able to claim an expense for a portion of the total amount you spent in the first year.

"But this year—the year you bought all these assets—you can't claim the full $30,000 as an expense. So we have to move the $30,000 that you recorded as an expense over to the balance sheet. That's why your profit is now $20,000. We will be able to record a much smaller amount as an expense for 'depreciation.'"

Jerry shook his head and said, "George, I really don't like this at all. This makes no sense. I spent $30,000 this year so why can't I claim it as an expense this year?"

"You will be claiming the $30,000 as an expense, slowly over time, over the next many years instead of all in this first year.

"Jerry, look, to be fair, on the one hand, this system does make sense in one respect. It is true, from a purely academic and theoretical perspective, that the office renovations, furniture and computers that were purchased will provide value for a long period of time, perhaps many years.

"Therefore, it would seem, at first glance, in order to provide a more accurate financial statement, that the decrease in value of these assets over time be recorded as an expense in the income statement each year. This is logical and makes sense from an accounting or financial statement perspective. When public companies release their audited financial statements, they are obligated by IFRS—sorry, that's International Financial Reporting Standards—to record their assets in very specific ways according to these principles. So I do agree that it is logical from a financial statement presentation perspective.

"So if you were presenting your financial statements for your business to someone who was interested in buying your business, they would want to see an accurate balance sheet showing the value of the assets your business owns, which includes the office furniture and computers."

Jerry interjected, "George, I am not selling my business and my business is not a publicly traded company, so how does that help me?"

"I agree with you. Recording assets and depreciation only makes sense from a financial statement disclosure perspective.

"However, from a tax perspective, it makes no sense, especially for a small-business owner. You spent $30,000 this year. That money is out of your bank account, it's gone. And yet, the government expects you to re-calculate your income based on theoretical financial statement accounting principles. The more reasonable approach would be for small-business owners to have their taxes payable calculated based on their cash flow and ability to pay.

"The idea of the income tax being based on one's ability to pay is critical. Income means the money came in. Income equals in … come, incoming. The money came in so, therefore, you can pay a percentage of that money that you now have, as tax.

"However, with the system of capitalizing assets and then depreciating over a period of time, the small-business owner is not being taxed on income and ability to pay. You lost $10,000 this year but are expected to pay tax as if you earned $20,000 of profit.

"Does this make any logical sense from a tax perspective? Obviously not! Yet, this is the actual system in place that small-business owners and self-employed sole proprietors must use to calculate their taxes payable.

"It is completely irrational and totally unfair from a tax perspective. It does not make any sense at all but this is the law and the CRA requirements are very clear on this.

"I would strongly approve a new system for small-business owners to completely abolish the requirement to record capital assets and depreci-ation for calculating taxes payable. Every small-business owner and self-employed individual should be permitted to deduct as an expense any and every amount they actually pay out during the year! This would be simple, easy and fair.

"So, Jerry, if you purchase $30,000 of office equipment, computers and renovations, you should be able to claim the entire amount as an expense in the actual year of purchase. The government obviously hates this idea because it would mean they would collect less tax in the short run. But this would ensure that income taxes are based on the ability to pay based on actual cash coming into the company.

"Honestly, these politicians and government bureaucrats who make these rules need to understand the cash flow reality of small-business owners.

"Jerry, you are not my only client who has this issue. Many clients complain to me that they owe income tax at the end of the year in years in which they make large asset purchases. They are still obligated to pay all their tax installments on time even if they have little or no cash on hand due to making capital investments in their business.

"The current system is really unfair, punitive, too complicated and makes no logical sense. I hereby beg our government to allow all small-business owners and self-employed individuals to no longer have to deal with this nonsense of capitalizing and depreciating assets. Recording all capital assets as full expenses in the year of purchase would simplify small-business owners' lives, simplify their tax return filings, make it easier for them in terms of their cash flow and be a common-sense policy."

"George, you are reasonable and sensible. I wish your proposals would become government policy. Of course, taxes payable should be calculated based on ability to pay as opposed to fancy theoretical accounting principles."

"Yes exactly. Accrual based accounting is not a logical basis to use for calculating our tax bills."

Jerry said, "What does accrual mean? What are you talking about?"

"Jerry, let me tell you a true story about 'accrual accounting.' I remember when I was in high school in my Grade 12 accounting class. The teacher, a really nice woman who I really liked, was trying to teach us about 'accrual accounting.'

"She was trying very hard but I had trouble understanding what she was saying. I asked her 'what does accrual mean?' I wanted to know the actual definition of the word. She replied, 'It means to accrue!'

"I said, 'You can't use the word in the definition!' I really failed to understand. Eventually, she was able to explain it to us.

"Accrual accounting refers to recording transactions in a year even if the cash relating to those transactions was not received or flowed out during that particular year.

"Jerry, in your case, this means that you must record the depreciation expense on the capital assets over many years even though the cash all left your bank account in the first year. Similarly, remember how you have to pay GST out to the government even before you collect it? That is also an example of accrual accounting.

"Including in your income amounts of revenue that you haven't even collected yet is accrual accounting. It means you sent out an invoice to a customer, therefore, you must record that invoice in revenue, even if the customer doesn't pay you until the following year. Accounts receivable, depreciation, accounts payable—these are all examples of accrual accounting.

"Accrual accounting does in fact make sense from an accounting and financial statement perspective. It does paint a more accurate picture of your financial position.

"But from a tax perspective, regarding your ability to pay income tax, it makes zero sense at all.

"How are you expected to pay income tax on income you have not received yet? How are you expected to pay income tax on an imaginary profit because you are forced to 'capitalize' assets instead of recording them as expenses?

"Now, some people will play devil's advocate and say accrual accounting also allows you to claim expenses and accounts payable. For example, let's say you made purchases or have bills to pay that relate to work done in December but you don't pay the bills until January, you can still record those as expenses in the income statement for December even though you don't pay the bills until the following year."

"Well, I don't have any such amounts so I'm out of luck!"

George went on, "The bottom line is it is not fair to apply income tax to income that was not received in physical reality or to apply income tax on imaginary accounting profits.

"My clients have complained about this to me over and over again. I have to tell them that I completely agree with them, it makes no sense, it's unfair, it's very difficult for the small-business owner in terms of their cash flow and politicians and policy makers who come up with these rules are out of touch with the reality of what the small-business owner goes through.

"I hereby strongly propose that small-business owners be permitted to use the 'cash basis' of accounting in order to calculate their taxes payable.

"This would mean that small-business owners would no longer have to include accounts receivable in their income, and their revenue would be calculated, very simply, as cash that was collected during the year. It is simply unfair, complex and illogical to maintain the current system for the small-business owner."[68]

"George, once again, I agree with you. I've had enough for today. If you'll excuse me."

Jerry stood up and headed to the door.

"Jerry, you are not excused, please sit down. You have now experienced first-hand all the bureaucracy, irrationality and unfairness inherent in the Canadian tax regime for small-business owners—corporate tax returns, GST returns, T4 filings for salaries and the personal tax return. On top of that, there are corporate tax installments, GST installments and payroll source deduction remittances to deal with. No wonder small-business owners end up paying a lot of penalties and interest for mistakes, late payments and late filings. A massive simplification of this entire regime is required at once."

Jerry said, "George, I know what you're about to say. You're going to propose some colossal fix to this bureaucratic nightmare of a tax system, right?"

Jerry sat down and waited for George to continue.

"Yes, exactly. I hereby propose that if someone is a small-business owner operating through a corporation, they should have only *one* tax return to file, just like a self-employed individual. The corporation can remain a separate legal entity for legal purposes, but have a simpler tax filing structure to reduce red tape, bureaucracy, accounting fees and frustrations for small-business owners.

"If we move to the cash basis of accounting for small-business owners, then the corporate tax return can be substantially simplified into a one-page income statement.

"This one-page income statement would be included in the personal tax return of the owner just as if they were self-employed.

"The amount of GST collected would be included in this one page as well, such that a GST return would no longer be necessary to file.

"And the owner's salary would show up on the corporate income statement as an expense and be included in the personal income of the owner, removing any requirement to file a T4 or open a CRA payroll account or pay source deductions from the corporation. This assumes they have no other employees.

"The corporate income tax, GST payable and personal income tax can all be combined into one tax payment in order to make things easier for the small-business owner.

"If we followed the above formula, small-business owners, who own and manage their own businesses, would save money on annual accounting and tax filing fees, would save a huge amount of time due to having less onerous and fewer tax filings and payments to make, and would also save a ton of penalties and interest for late filing and late payments.

"It would also mean I would pretty much lose all my revenue and have to find a new job, as would many other accountants!"

Jerry could only dream that his tax filings would become that easy. He stopped George from continuing as he couldn't handle any more of this for one day.

TIP #26 — *Don't Assume Anything*

I will never forget the following story. It was my first ever job as an accounting articling student. I had no idea what I was doing and was unable to do any work. Sadly, university did not prepare us for the actual job. In response to my boss asking me why I did something in a particular way I said, "Well, I guess I just assumed." And he replied, "When you assume, you make an a** out of you and me."

When it comes to taxes for someone who is self-employed or a small-business owner, you can never assume anything based on logic or intuition. The Canadian tax system is counter-intuitive, illogical and nonsensical. You might want to follow the opposite of your instincts as if you are living in some sort of bizarro world.

With regards to making adjustments at year-end for tax purposes for your business, whether as a sole proprietor, self-employed individual or in a corporation, you must use the silly system of accrual-based accounting. Even though this is unfair from a taxes payable perspective, the law is the law. So until we put enough pressure on the Prime Minister and Minister of Finance to change these laws as they relate to the self-employed and small-business owner, be prepared to be pay tax based on a calculation of income that is not related to your cash flow position.

Chapter 20

THE GOLDEN YEARS

When Jerry reached the ripe age of 60 years Elaine threw him a really nice surprise party. Everyone was there, including his children, his loyal employees and, of course, his favourite accountant, George.

Everyone was having a really great time at the party. There was music playing, people were eating and drinking, and everyone was going up to Jerry and offering their good wishes.

Strangely, George was sitting in a corner, by himself, slouched over, looking at the food on his plate. He had aged quite a bit over his long career and his hair, what was left of it, was now pure gray. He didn't look happy; in fact, he looked quite grumpy.

Jerry noticed this out of the corner of his eye and went over to George to see what was wrong.

"George, what's the matter? Why so grumpy? It's a birthday party, cheer up!"

"Jerry, you're 60 years old now. It's a great milestone. I'm happy for you, even if I'm not showing it outwardly. But now we need to discuss your retirement planning."

"Is that what's making you grumpy?"

"Yes, Jerry. Yes. RRSP, TFSA, RRIF, CPP, OAS, GIS, estate planning, deemed disposition at date of death, T3 trust returns after death, ..."

Jerry interrupted, "George, stop. Just stop right now. You're making me grumpy. I have no idea what you just said; all of that was complete gibberish to me. It's my birthday party and I demand you cheer up. We can discuss those things another time."

George relented. He got up from his seat; he cheered himself up and began to enjoy the party.

The next day, Jerry and George met to talk about retirement planning.

Jerry began, "George, I don't know why you insisted on this meeting. What do I have to worry about? I put away money in my RRSP and TFSA, and I paid into CPP all those years I was working. Won't I also receive Old Age Security—yes, I know that one—OAS?"

"Yes, I'm sure you'll be financially secure but even with a Registered Retirement Savings Plan, Canada Pension Plan, Old Age Security and other benefits that help senior citizens, the entire system is complicated and we still have some planning to do.

"First, let's start with the CPP. Since you contributed the maximum amount into CPP for most of your working years, you will receive the maximum pension, which is $1,175 per month."[69]

"That's it? Only $14,100 per year? That's hardly enough to live off."

"Correct, the CPP is not meant to fund all your living expenses during retirement. It is meant to help supplement your living expenses. $14,100 per year assumes you start receiving CPP at age 65. Keep in mind, CPP also has some disability benefits and some survivor benefits to your spouse and children up to a certain age. Your spouse won't receive the same amount as you would have received but it's still something.

"Don't forget to apply for CPP. You are not enrolled automatically. There have been cases where people have paid into CPP their entire working life, neglected to apply and never received any CPP because they didn't know they had to apply."

"George, are you joking?"

"Sadly, no, I am not joking."

"What about OAS? Must I also apply for OAS?"

"Good question. OAS is separate from CPP. You will be enrolled automatically in this program so you don't need to apply. However, some people are not eligible for automatic enrollment so they must apply. If you are automatically enrolled, you will receive a letter from the government the month after you turn 64 years old. If you don't receive this letter, then you need to apply in writing.

"OAS is paid out by the government from general government revenue. The maximum you can receive is approximately $7,300 for the year."[70]

Jerry was adding it up in his head. "Okay, so I will receive $14,100 from CPP and $7,300 from OAS, so that's $21,400. Aren't there other goodies for senior citizens? I always hear in the news that once someone turns 65, there are lots of nice juicy tax benefits."

"Yes. We need to look at everything together.

"There is the Guaranteed Income Supplement—the GIS. This is a tax-free benefit paid out to anyone over the age of 65 who earns below $18,600 of income. These are tax-free payments to ensure that senior citizens are not living in poverty and are able to afford their monthly living expenses. Your income will be too high to receive this."

"Okay, so that won't apply to me but I'm glad that it exists to help those individuals with lower incomes."

"You will be eligible for some extra tax credits like the 'age amount' and the 'pension income' amount. These will reduce your tax payable each year."

"Sounds good. Are we almost done?"

"Are we almost done? Of course not! Jerry, what are your plans for the next 10 years? You are 60 years old now. Are you going to retire at 65 or 70 or 75? Are you going to work forever? Do you have any idea of what you want to do?"

"Well, to be honest, I'm not really sure. I'd like to keep working and running the business, or at least transition out and retire slowly over time."

"The reason I ask is because if you continue working and taking a salary from the business, this will push you into a higher tax bracket once you start receiving your CPP and OAS. In fact, if you hit an income of $79,000,[71] your OAS will begin to be 'clawed back.' Once you hit income of $128,000,[72] you will lose your OAS entirely. So we have to ensure, if you care about receiving OAS, that your income stays under those levels."

"So you're saying I should work less and deliberately earn less income in my 60s in order to receive OAS from the government."

"Well, all I am saying is, if you want to maximize the amount of government benefits you receive to fund your living expenses, as opposed to using your own money, then you must show a level of income that is less than $79,000. But we have to be careful, as always, because, you have a large balance accumulated in your RRSP."

"What's wrong with having a large RRSP? I thought it's a good thing to save money!"

"Well, remember that every dollar you withdraw from your RRSP is included in your income and you will have to pay tax on those withdrawals."

"Okay, so I will just leave the money in the RRSP until the day I die and I will continue working."

George laughed. "Jerry, that's not how it works. Once you turn 71 years old, the RRSP turns into a Registered Retirement Income Fund, known as a RRIF, and the money starts coming out at rates prescribed by the government, whether you like it or not."

"Wait, what do you mean, the money starts coming out automatically when I turn 71? I don't have any choice in the matter."

"Well, there is an exception if you hold 'annuities' in your RRIF. Annuities are like insurance policies that pay you set amounts at set times. But if you don't buy annuities in your RRIF, then there are minimum required withdrawals."

"What if I decide to keep working well past the age of 71 and not retire and don't need the money from my RRSP?"

"You're out of luck. This is a major problem with the RRSP system. It was designed in a time when life expectancies were a lot shorter. Today, some people don't retire right away, at 65. They wait until they are a bit older. Or they continue to work part time or consult on the side. Some people never retire because they feel that continuing to work in some form or another keeps their bodies and minds healthy and invigorated."

"Wow. I guess this system made sense in the old days when things were simpler and most people retired at age 65. But today, this seems very outdated."

"Yes, it is very outdated and way too complicated. The RRSP system was created in 1957 when the average life expectancy was between 65 and 75 years old.[73] RRSPs and RRIFs are too complicated. Mistakes can be made easily.

"I had a client who was over 85 years old. Everyone knows once someone turns 71 they can no longer contribute to their RRSP. Unfortunately, this woman suffered because of an error on the part of her bank advisor.

"This bank advisor made an RRSP contribution for her of $15,000 because she noticed she had RRSP contribution room! I couldn't believe it. This elderly woman on a fixed income was assessed several thousand dollars in penalties by the CRA for the over-contribution.

"It was an absolute nightmare to have everything reversed and corrected and the penalties refunded. This is a perfect example of a complex tax system having unintended consequences and really hurting average people, including elderly citizens on low incomes who have to spend time, money, effort and undergo stress to fix their ridiculous tax problems."

"Wow, that is crazy. George, I know you will never let that happen to me."

"Of course I would never let anything like that happen to you. Now, let's talk about your TFSAs."

"George, you will be proud of me. I have been maximizing my and Elaine's TFSA contributions for many years."

"Well done, Jerry."

"Please don't tell me the TFSA is like the RRSP and when I turn 71 minimum withdrawals will begin?"

"Thankfully, the TFSA is more flexible. You can withdraw money at any time for any reason without worrying about any penalties or taxes payable. The withdrawals from the TFSA are not included in your income and you don't pay tax on them."

"Okay, so I should start emptying my TFSA today?"

"No, no, no, no, no! Do not empty out your TFSA!"

"Then what should I do? Should I retire right now and begin withdrawing from my RRSP? Or should I keep working and delay my RRSP withdrawals until I turn 70? Or any combination thereof? I feel like my head is starting to spin."

"Yes, Jerry, welcome to my head-spinning world. There is not one Canadian who can figure this out on their own. Unless you are an actuary or perhaps an accountant, this is an extremely difficult system to navigate.

"Let's not forget about pension income splitting. Once Elaine starts earning her pension, she can split some of that with you. Whoever is in a higher tax bracket can split some of their pension income with the spouse with the lower income. So that will help minimize your tax bill. The spouse with the higher income can also apply to have some of their CPP taxed in the lower-income spouse's tax return.

"Remember any medical expenses that are not covered by the government or your insurance can be claimed as a medical expense on your tax return.

"Don't forget about the 'Disability Tax Credit' which who knows, maybe one day you can qualify for depending on your medical situation."

"George, I'm still not clear on what to do."

"Jerry, you will start receiving your CPP and OAS when you turn 65. If you are still able and willing to work, then continue doing so. If you don't want to continue working, then stop working and start taking RRSP withdrawals so your tax bill upon death will be minimized. Alternatively, you can fund your early retirement from now until 71 with the money from CPP, OAS and other investments you have in your non-registered accounts. This way, your RRSP can continue to grow to fund your later years of retirement.

"The ultimate goal for retirement planning in Canada has become a game of minimizing income tax and maximizing government benefits. In order to accomplish this goal, people try to keep their taxable income as low as possible. This will ensure they pay as little tax as possible and also receive as many government benefits as possible. They want to smooth out their income so they never hit too high of a tax bracket, especially in the year of death."

George took a deep breath and sighed. Jerry could sense the exasperation.

"Jerry, I wish that this entire conversation we just had was unnecessary."

"What do you mean?"

"Well, as you can see, the retirement system is extremely complicated. There is hardly one Canadian who can figure this out on their own. The government has made the system way too complicated. CPP, OAS, GIS, TFSA, RRSP, RRIF. The government wants people to save money. They think, in their infinite wisdom, that if they don't create these savings vehicles then we won't save any money. I think their goal is noble. The government should, in fact, encourage people to save money. But I wish there would be a simpler way."

"So what do you have in mind?"

"Well, I have a grand master plan to fix this mess. It would have to be implemented slowly over time, maybe over five to ten years, but once fully implemented, it would make saving money and retirement planning way simpler."

Jerry was intrigued.

"First of all, I would eliminate RESPs, RRSPs, RRIFs and TFSA accounts. Just eliminate them completely. Every single one of them. Goodbye RESPs. Goodbye RRSPs. Goodbye RRIFs. Goodbye TFSAs.

"These accounts are too complicated. Some people, but not all, are of the opinion that these accounts only help those who are already wealthy and able to save money, and do nothing to help those Canadians who are unable to even start to put money aside. The accounts have contribution limits that people frequently exceed due to misunderstanding the rules, generating outrageous amounts of penalties and interest. Overall, these accounts are complicated, costly to administer and very confusing for the average taxpayer. The typical Canadian ends up paying professional advisors to guide them on which accounts to contribute to and how much to contribute into each account. These advisors can often make mistakes in their recommendations. It's a no-win situation."

"But George, without these accounts, there would be no incentive for people to save money for their future and people would be taxed on all their investment income."

"Jerry, even now, with all these accounts, only 35% of Canadian households pay into an RRSP and 40% contribute to a TFSA.[74] So my point is that there are still too many Canadian households that are not contributing to their RRSPs or TFSAs. So perhaps a better system could be designed. Perhaps if a simpler system would be in place, more people would utilize it."

"What do you have in mind?"

"Well, one idea could be to do nothing."

"George, what do you mean nothing?"

"I mean, nothing."

"But George, I don't understand. Don't you want people to save money? Don't you think we have to do something?"

"Yes, of course. But why is it the government's job to create a complicated, impossible-to-understand retirement savings program for individual Canadians. The government is always trying to do something. For once, let's try doing nothing. For example let's educate children from a young age in school about the importance of saving money. Let's eliminate income tax on the first $50,000 of income, as I have described before, so Canadians can keep more of their hard-earned pay cheques, which will allow them to save more for their futures. You see, even nothing is something."

"George, I don't know if I like that idea. I think people need a bit more motivation and encouragement to save money."

"Okay, Jerry. Then, how about the following? Remember before I said that we should allow every individual to earn $50,000 of income free of tax?"

"Yes, of course. I love that idea. Eliminate all tax deductions and credits and make up for it by lowering the tax rate, right?"

"Exactly. So one way we can encourage people to save money for their future is by educating them that when they retire and begin to live off their investment income, their first $50,000 of income is tax free, and that includes investment income as well. If people realize, in retirement, they will pay zero tax on their first $50,000 of investment income, they will be incentivized to save money for their retirement."

"That's interesting, George. But won't these retirees also be receiving CPP from the government, pushing them into an income bracket above $50,000 possibly, and then they would start paying tax?"

"Wow, Jerry, you have learned a lot from all our conversations, haven't you? I'm very proud of you. That's a good point. So another option—which I dislike but I, reluctantly and under protest, will offer—is to replace the RESPs, RRSPs, RRIFs and TFSAs with one simple, easy-to-understand account. To keep it simple, we can just call it the CSA, the Canada Savings Account.

"This account would have complete flexibility in regards to contributions and withdrawals. There would be no annual contribution limits and no required withdrawals at any age. Contributions would not be a deduction on the tax return and withdrawals would be tax free. The account would be most similar to a TFSA. There would be a lifetime contribution limit instead of annual limits, which will eliminate the possibility of people incurring frustrating over-contribution penalties due to the very complicated rules that exist currently.

"We need to design a retirement system in such a way that people are no longer encouraged to try to show as little income as possible on their tax return to generate the maximum amount of government benefits and pay the least amount of income tax.

"We need to find a way to encourage people to save money for their retirement but without all the intense complexity, confusion and unintended consequences that we currently have."

Jerry liked this idea. "That sounds very interesting but what about CPP, OAS and GIS?"

"Well, if Canadians agree they like the Canada Pension Plan, then we should keep it. We can keep contributing into it and keep receiving the payouts. However, the flaws of the CPP must be fixed. People who have paid into CPP should be automatically enrolled to receive their benefits to avoid the sad situations where people who fail to apply don't receive their CPP.

"The Old Age Security system should simply be combined into the Guaranteed Income Supplement (GIS) system to make it simpler, as I have described before, and remove the need for a lot of complicated tax planning. There are senior citizens who desperately, every year, try to keep their income below $79,000 so they receive the full amount of OAS, or at least keep their income under $129,000 so they receive some OAS. This is just silly and complicated. The OAS payments are taxable and included in income, which doesn't really make sense. After all, if the government claims that senior citizens require money to be secure in their old age, then doesn't that mean they can't afford to pay income tax on it? The government spends $50.6 billion on the OAS and GIS combined.[75] Why not take the money that is currently spent on OAS, and simply combine it with the GIS, make it tax free and redirect it to those who need it the most. Along with abolishing income tax on the first $50,000 of income as I have described before, this would go a long way to make things a lot simpler and easier for retirement planning."

"So under your plan, it seems like the only planning I would need to do to retire is figure out how much money I need every year and then calculate how much savings I would need to accumulate to fund that lifestyle."

"Exactly."

"Okay, George, I now have a splitting headache from all of this, so thank you very much."

Jerry loved George's ideas but unfortunately George's dream was not yet reality. On his way home, he stopped to buy some Advil to help with his headache.

TIP #27 — *It's Complicated*

For proper retirement planning, first of all, start saving money when you're young, if you can. Even small amounts add up over time due to compounding interest. There are some great books about this topic. I have listed some of them in the Resources section at the back of this book.

If you are in your 50s or early 60s and have not yet met with an accountant, fee-only certified financial planner or other such advisor, then I highly recommend you do so, to start retirement planning early. You will need to decide when to take CPP and OAS, and when to start withdrawing from your RRSP and TFSA. It's important to come up with a plan.

Be wary of advisors who receive a commission for certain products that they sell you. You must be proactive and ask explicitly "What is your fee structure?" "Do you earn a commission or do I pay you a flat fee for your advice?"

The main points to remember are that you don't want to be in too high a tax bracket in retirement. If your taxable income reaches $79,054 (2020 figure), then you start to lose out on your OAS payments. Once your taxable income reaches $128,137 (2020 figure), then you lose your OAS entirely.

If you amass too much in your RRSP, it may still be worth it, but be prepared for tax bills in your retirement and upon death. The TFSA offers much more flexibility, so if you can, always maximize both your TFSA and RRSP.

Don't forget about pension income splitting from the higher-income spouse to the lower-income spouse.

Don't forget to apply for the CPP and OAS. You will not be enrolled automatically in CPP and possibly OAS as well.

The Disability Tax Credit can be very valuable. There is no age restriction to be eligible for this credit. I have listed the CRA link about the Disability Tax Credit on the Resources pages.

The bottom line is you will most likely need someone to look at your specific financial and tax situation and determine a course of action based on your own individual specific circumstances.

Chapter 21

DEATH AND TAXES—THERE IS NO ESCAPE

Many years passed. George had retired and handed over his practice to his very capable, intelligent daughter, Delores. She was a great accountant, not nearly as grumpy as her father, and quickly developed relationships with her father's clients as well as their adult children.

One day, Delores received a panicked phone call from Jerry's son, Soda.

"Delores, you won't believe what happened. My father received a letter from the CRA addressed to his estate!"

"Soda, did your father pass away?"

"No! He's totally alive. I'm sitting here with him right now and we're in shock. His CPP and OAS payments have stopped. This is a disaster! What do we do?"

"Calm down. We will simply inform CRA of the error and straighten everything out. I will take care of it for you. But don't feel like you're the only one in this situation. Back in March of 2017, a man from New Brunswick received a letter from the CRA addressed to his estate. And like your father, this man was very much alive. The CRA, for some reason, had him on file as deceased![76]

"The CBC once reported that 319 people were declared dead by the CRA between January 1, 2016, and December 31, 2017, even though they were all living![77] This was considered an improvement because in the previous two-year period from January 1, 2014, to December 31, 2015, 524 people were mistakenly proclaimed dead.

"The problem, of course, is once the CRA files someone as dead, all the benefits that they are entitled to cease, causing problems for the person who is still alive. Obviously, when they try to file their tax return, they will run into other problems as well."

"Delores, that is absolutely ridiculous. I trust you will fix this for us. Thanks for your help."

Some time went by, Jerry's status was reinstated to "alive" and he continued receiving his CPP and OAS benefits. Jerry was now well into his old age and Elaine was, sadly, very ill. He, their children and grandchildren were gathered around in the hospital room. Elaine was peacefully lying down in the bed. Their eldest child, Soda, who was now dealing with all of Jerry and Elaine's tax issues, called Delores to ask if she could visit.

Delores walked into the room. She saw Jerry sitting by the bed, holding Elaine's hand. All of Jerry and Elaine's children and grandchildren were in the room watching over Elaine and ensuring all her needs were being taken care of.

Delores had guided Jerry and Elaine through their retirement planning. Jerry finally retired from his business at the age of 75. He sold his business and the proceeds from the sale helped fund a comfortable retirement for him and Elaine.

They were able to enjoy meeting their grandchildren, watching them grow up and even attend some of their grandchildren's weddings.

Delores greeted everyone in the room. Jerry was too focused on Elaine to engage in conversation so Soda asked Delores, "Delores, we need to know about everything in regards to taxes when my mom eventually passes."

"Soda, there is a lot to worry about and consider, but don't worry, I will explain everything to you and help you along. For now, spend time with your family and we will deal with each issue as it comes up."

Delores left so Jerry and his family could be together in Elaine's final moments.

A few weeks later, Delores received the news that Elaine had passed away. Delores began the tax work and filings required as a result of the death of a taxpayer.

She immediately called Soda and told him to contact Service Canada and the CRA as soon as possible to inform them of the death. This would ensure that all CPP and OAS payments would stop immediately.

Soda did as Delores suggested. He also asked Delores to not involve his father in any of the tax work required for Elaine's passing. He didn't want to burden his father with any additional stress at this difficult time in his life.

Soda ended up spending an hour or so on the phone with Service Canada and was told to send in a copy of the death certificate. He asked Delores if that was really necessary.

Delores explained to him that he should obtain at least ten copies of the death certificate, perhaps even more, in order to provide these to the CRA, Service Canada, the banks and other financial institutions, and lawyers that will require them.

She also told him, "Soda, I am e-mailing you a form that you need to fill out. This is to apply for the CPP death benefit."

Soda was weary of filling out another form. "How much is the CPP death benefit?"

"$2,500 but it's taxable. The amount will be included in income in Elaine's estate return or in the tax return of a beneficiary. So probably close to half of it will be paid back in tax."

Soda let out a loud groan and continued, "Delores, my siblings and I received a life insurance payout because my mom had a life insurance policy. Do we have to pay tax on the life insurance proceeds we receive?"

"Soda, life insurance proceeds are tax free so no need to report those amounts in your tax returns or pay tax on those amounts."

"Well, that's a relief. Finally, some good news."

Delores began to prepare Elaine's last personal tax return (referred to as the "final tax return"), which must be filed upon death. This proved difficult as it took a lot of time and effort to gather all the appropriate T slips from the banks and the government. Delores hated when clients died for the obvious reasons, but also because it was very complicated and a lot of work to make sure everything was being done properly.

A few weeks later, Delores was at work when she received a call from Soda. "Delores, my father took a turn for the worse and is now in the hospital."

Delores was sad to hear this news. Jerry was one of her favourite clients.

Jerry's son went to visit his father every day in the hospital. One day, while Jerry was watching TV, another patient was rolled into the empty bed beside him.

Jerry immediately recognized the frail old man who would become his new roommate. It was his favourite grumpy accountant, George.

Jerry looked over at him and George recognized Jerry as well. They smiled and greeted each other warmly.

They hadn't spoken in many years as George's daughter was doing a fine job and his services were no longer required.

George looked calm, serene and happy. It was the first time Jerry saw George looking so happy.

"Jerry, you look surprised to see me. Did you think I would live forever? Did you think I would never get sick and end up in the hospital?"

Jerry smiled, "I'm surprised because you don't look grumpy!"

"That's because I've been retired for the past 20 years. Of course I'm no longer grumpy."

Although they were in the hospital, they felt relieved to be together once again and they agreed to never discuss anything related to taxes in their final days together.

One day, Delores, along with Soda, came to visit.

Everyone greeted each other and they began talking.

Delores said, "Dad, I have been discussing some of the tax implications of death with Jerry's son. He doesn't believe anything I said. It was a bit simpler when Elaine passed away because her assets passed directly to

Jerry. But now, it's more complicated because Jerry is the last surviving spouse. I need you to tell him that everything I'm saying is true."

Jerry and his son were listening intently and as she said these words, George immediately became grumpy once again. The life had seemed to vacate his face and body but he began talking.

George said, "It's true, it's all true. Death and taxes, you can never escape."

Jerry said, "What do you mean? If I'm dead, I'm dead. What tax implications are there by dying? Who cares what happens when I die? I'll be dead!"

George said, "Well, not according to the CRA!"

"Oh no! What can you possibly mean by that? George, I thought I was done. I thought I was in the clear. I am leaving this world in peace. What possible tax implications could there be?"

Soda had done a good job of shielding Jerry from all the tax work required as a result of Elaine's passing.

George said, "On the date of death, the CRA considers all assets owned by the deceased to have been sold at fair market value and a capital gain must be reported and included in income.

"So, for example, Jerry, all of your investment accounts that hold stocks and bonds, any real estate or any business you own, all of these will be considered to be sold on the day you die."

"But I'm not planning to sell these. Don't they just transfer to my children?"

George said, grumpily, "No. Absolutely not. When Elaine died, all her assets transferred directly to you because you were married and the accounts were held jointly. But since you are the last surviving spouse, the assets are considered to be sold.

"This is known as the 'deemed disposition' because they are 'deemed' to have been 'disposed' of. This often results in complex calculations that your son and Delores will have to do to determine the original cost of the assets, and what the current fair market value would be.

"For some assets it is difficult to figure out a fair market value, such as shares in a private corporation or real estate that has not actually been sold. There is some subjectivity involved and often expert valuators must be hired to come up with a correct value, which is yet another added expense for the taxpayer."

Jerry's son interrupted, "Are you sure this is correct, George? How can people pay capital gains on assets that have not actually been sold in reality? No gain was actually realized so where is the money supposed to come from to pay the tax?"

"It's a mystery! I do not understand it! Sometimes I think I am crazy and the tax system actually is logical but then I think about rules like these, and I wonder. Has the whole world gone mad or is it just me? Why do we allow such a system? Why do we tolerate it?

"When someone dies, it's bad enough the family has to deal with the death of a loved one, they now must deal with a huge tax bill.

"Even after the final tax return is filed, and the capital gains tax is paid on the deemed sale of assets that haven't actually been sold, then there is the matter of income that the 'estate' continues to earn after the date of death.

"The 'estate' refers to the assets and investments that the deceased person owned that continue to generate income after death. Each year, the estate (until it is settled) must file a special tax return, called a 'T3'—the trust return—to show all the income earned every year from the investments. The T3 pays tax on the income of this deceased person from beyond the grave.

"I always tell people, don't worry, and don't be sad that your loved one died. They will live on as they continue to pay income tax from the great beyond. Even after death, one continues to pay tax every year as long as there continues to be income and until the estate is settled. That's essentially what a T3 return is; it's a tax return for a dead person.

"We should call it what it is without the use of euphemisms. We should rename the 'trust' return to the 'Completely 100% Dead and Buried No Longer Alive Taxpayer Continuing to Pay Tax from Beyond the Grave Tax' return. The T3 return is due on March 31st for the previous year ending December 31st. The problem is that estates often receive T3 slips that may not arrive until the first week of April. So we are forced to file the T3 return on March 31st to avoid a late-filing penalty and then file an amended return in April to reflect the additional slips."

George paused and took a deep breath. He looked at Jerry. He looked at Jerry's son. He looked over at Delores and signaled for her to approach him. She came very close to him and he handed her a letter that was sealed in an envelope. The envelope said "To be read at my funeral."

He looked at Delores one last time lovingly, he looked over at Jerry and frowned grumpily, and then he closed his eyes forever.

TIP #28 — *Estate Planning*

Get a will! Whatever you do, you must get a will and keep it up to date. Go see an estate and wills lawyer right now.

If you have any assets, such as investments or your own business, there will be tax implications at death, so plan ahead, as always. Plan, plan, plan. Find an accountant or tax advisor who is knowledgeable and specializes in estate planning. Estate freezes, estate planning, T3 trust returns, the final tax return, it can all get very complicated and the rules are constantly changing, so find someone who is up to date and able to advise you.

You should have "beneficiaries" named on all insurance and other such policies, as well as on all your bank accounts, savings accounts, investment accounts and registered accounts (TFSA, RRSP, RRIF, etc.).

All property (bank accounts, investment accounts, etc.) should be held jointly with both spouses, so that when the first spouse dies, all assets are transferred to the surviving spouse without a deemed disposition resulting in a capital gain.

When the last surviving spouse dies, then all assets (aside from the TFSA) will be deemed to have been sold and a capital gain must be reported and capital gains tax will be payable.

If someone dies and you are responsible for the filing of their final tax return, the due dates are specific.

- If the death occurred between January and October, the due date is April 30th of the next year.
- If the death occurred between November and December, the due date is six months from the date of death.

Chapter 22

My Dream for the Future

George's funeral had a great turn out. All his clients showed up from near and far. He requested in his will that The Beatles' song, "The Taxman," be played to open his funeral. A small band, seated in front of the grave, played the song beautifully. People in the crowd were chuckling and giggling at this but they knew this was the perfect song for George's farewell.

George's daughter Delores delivered a moving eulogy. She described her father as someone who was hard working, dedicated to his clients and, although he seemed grumpy, he was in fact very cheerful, jovial and happy when he wasn't working.

As she neared the end of her eulogy, she explained that her father handed her a letter that he requested be read at this time.

She opened the letter and began reading.

"I hope you're all having a great time at my funeral. It must be strange to have to listen to a speech by a dead guy but I knew this was the only way I could ensure I would be heard without all of you constantly interrupting me.

"First of all, thanks for coming today. I know that no one likes going to funerals. They are awkward, strange and force us to come to terms with our own mortality.

"I'd like you all to know that I died a happy man. Although I may have seemed grumpy, I did enjoy working with all of you for all those years. I feel I have, in fact, contributed to society by helping all of you navigate a complicated tax system.

"My last dying wish is to challenge all of you to make an effort to fulfill my dream.

"This dream has unfortunately gone unfulfilled in my lifetime. I am hoping that you, all of you here today who took the time to come to my funeral, will heed the following message, and let these words penetrate your hearts and minds. I am hereby challenging you to help fulfill my dream.

"What is my dream?

"A simple tax system.

"I dream of the day when the Canadian tax system is so simple that we will no longer need to hire grumpy accountants or purchase any software to help us file our tax returns.

"I dream of the day when the Canadian tax system is so simple that the majority of people would not even have a requirement to file a tax return.

"I dream of the day when the Canadian tax system is so simple that no one would be required to keep any receipts, no one would ever receive a reassessment, no one would have a need to file an objection or an appeal and no one would have to go through a CRA audit.

"I dream of the day when the Canadian tax system is so simple that we will no longer need to spend $7 billion per year paying accountants and others to file our tax returns.

"I dream of the day when the Canadian tax system is so simple that we will no longer pay over $4 billion per year for the budget for the CRA.

"I dream of the day when the Canadian tax system is so simple that the CRA would no longer need to employ 40,000 people.[78]

"Is this dream unrealistic?

"Is this dream unfathomable?

"I think not.

"We can make this happen.

"In many other countries, this dream is already a reality.

"England, Denmark, Sweden, Estonia, Norway, Iceland, Spain, Finland, Israel and others have tax systems in which the majority of taxpayers, such as employees, do not have to file a tax return.

"We must put pressure on our politicians to make this a reality.

"Canada has not had comprehensive tax reform since the Carter Commission issued its report in 1967, over 50 years ago. Over half a century of a complicated and inefficient tax system is enough, in my humble opinion.

"What would the Canadian tax system look like if my dream came true?

"It would be quite simple.

"The first order of business would be to fix the individual T1 tax filing system. This would be done by abolishing every single tax deduction and tax credit.

"There would no longer be any requirement to file a tax return for employees. Under the current system, employees receive their T4 slips from their employer and the employer files the T4 slip with the CRA. All we have to do is end it there. Meaning, the T4 is the tax return. Since there are no deductions and no credits, the T4 becomes the tax return and it's already filed by the employer.

"The only people who would have to file tax returns would be self-employed individuals, business owners and those who earn capital gains.

"If the dream I just described becomes a reality, this would go a long way to making the lives of the majority of Canadians easier. No need to keep receipts, no need to file a tax return, no need to worry about CRA requesting copies of your receipts for an audit, no need to worry about unexpected tax bills, no need to spend money purchasing tax software or hiring an accountant.

"I dream of replacing the current complex system of myriad benefits, such as GST Credits, Canada Child Benefits, Old Age Security and the

Guaranteed Income Supplement, with a simple Guaranteed Minimum Income. People would be automatically enrolled in these programs based on their income from their T4 slip or, if they don't work or have income, there should be a very simple half-page form to file."

Delores took a breath. Everyone was still listening intently. She couldn't believe her father wrote all this down for her to read at the funeral but this was his dying wish, so she continued.

"Jerry, are you here? If you are still alive and sitting here listening, what about you and all the other small-business owners?

"The self-employed and small-business owners would still have to report their income to CRA even under my dream version of a simple tax system.

"The self-employment tax return can be one page. This return would give the self-employed two options to calculate their tax: gross revenue or net income.

"My dream is that the GST small supplier limit be increased from the current $30,000 to $100,000 and continue to increase each year with inflation. It is too costly, inefficient and burdensome for every little, average, ordinary, self-employed person to have to worry about being an unpaid tax collector under the GST regime. As an exemption limit, $30,000 is way too low and this limit has not increased with inflation since 1991.

"There is no reason why the GST return filing cannot be combined with an individual's personal tax return to avoid having to file yet another tax return. In fact, even the current T2125 Statement of Business or Professional Activities form requires the self-employed individual to enter their GST account number and amount of GST they collected! The CRA should simply collect the information from that form and consider that to be the GST return.

"For those small-business owners who have corporations, my dream is that they would be able to withdraw money from their businesses in a simple and easy manner without having to create complex CRA payroll accounts, deduct taxes from their pay at source and file T4 slips. They should be able to withdraw the money from their corporation, and show it as self-employment income on their tax return. This would be so much easier for them and result in the same tax revenue for the government. Under the current system, even paying a dividend from a corporation involves complicated calculations to determine if the dividend is 'eligible' or 'ineligible,' the gross-up amount and the dividend tax credit.

"I envision a type of tax filing where a small-business owner can have a corporation for legal liability purposes but have only one tax return to file that would combine both his corporate and personal tax filings. This would be similar to an S-Corp in the United States. The income statement of the corporation would simply be included on the individual's personal tax return so there is only one filing required.

"All self-employed people and small-business people should be able to calculate their tax based on the cash they actually collected in the year. No more accounts receivable, depreciation, accounts payable, inventory adjustments, etc. Cash in, cash out is how taxes payable should be calculated.

"This is my dream!

"What about investing and saving for retirement? Currently, we have RRSPs, RESPs, TFSAs, RRIFs, CPP, OAS and the list goes on. This is too complicated and costly. We should abolish the TFSA, abolish the RRSP, abolish RESPs, abolish RRIFs, abolish it all.

"This is my dream!

"In lieu of all those complicated nonsensical accounts, we can educate people to save from a young age, educate people that their first $50,000 of income is tax free, which would include investment income in retirement or simply have one tax-free account that can be used for any and all savings purposes as the individual sees fit. To keep it simple, there would be no annual contribution limits. Instead, a lifetime contribution limit will suffice.

"For those of us who fall in love and decide to get married, my dream is that you and your loved one would be taxed as a family unit, with the first $75,000 or $80,000 of family income being tax free.

"Each spouse would inform their employer of the amount of income the other spouse earns so that the employer can deduct the correct amount of pay based on combined family income. There would be no taxes payable or tax refund and no need to even file a tax return at the end of the year. The T4s are the tax returns!

"This is my dream and it is possible."

Delores paused again. She apologized to all the mourners for George's long-winded letter but they were all smiling and they knew that the best way to pay respect to their beloved grumpy accountant was to indulge his rants one last time.

Delores continued reading. "Do we really think that the government, politicians and bureaucrats should use the tax system to encourage and discourage behaviour? Do the politicians, bureaucrats and academics who come up with this insanely complicated tax system feel that the majority of Canadians are not smart enough to conduct their own lives in the best, healthiest way possible? They feel they must use the tax system to nudge us along and create a new tax deduction and tax credit for every life milestone and life event. But the system has become so complex that this nudging has too many unintended consequences.

"Our governments and politicians incurred over $1 trillion of debt[79] on our behalf but claim that they need to use the tax system to encourage us to be on our best behaviour!

"We all need to wake up and do some soul searching as a country. We must ask ourselves if we really need the federal government involved in these household decisions, which cause our tax system to become more complicated with time.

"Wouldn't my dream be easier and simpler?

"We don't have such an insane system with any other bill or payment that we make. Car insurance, home insurance, tenant's insurance, utility bills, phone bills, internet bills, you name it.

"These bills are usually very simple and easy to understand and calculated for us with no deductions or credits. There is nothing to 'file.'

"All you have to do is pay the amount showing on the bill. No filing obligations, no complicated calculations to do, doesn't cost you a penny, you don't have to hire a 'bill filing professional' and potentially have months and months or even years to claim your credits and deductions and go through potential litigation with the company.

"So why do we have such a system for our tax bills?

"If we fulfill my dream, Canadians would no longer be afraid of the government, no longer have to spend countless hours record keeping and bookkeeping, no longer have to keep receipts, no longer have to pay expensive accountants to help them file tax returns and no longer be audited by the CRA. They could simply run their lives and small businesses without fear and undue interference from government bureaucrats.

"If my dream came true, the CRA would no longer have a need to monitor Canadians' Facebook and Twitter accounts if it suspected those taxpayers were possibly cheating on their taxes.[80]

"My dream is for a simple tax system.

"Will you help make my dream come true?

"Even though I am no longer here, you are and you can make this happen.

"Contact your Member of Parliament, contact the Minister of Finance, contact the Prime Minister, ask your accountant to contact the CPA Canada tax committees with these ideas, and share this important message with all your family, friends and co-workers.

"It is time that all Canadians across this great land wake up and call for meaningful and comprehensive tax simplification.

"My dream can become reality but only if every Canadian helps to make it so.

"Will you wake up and take action?"

TIP #29 — *Wake Up and Take Action!*

The first 28 tips in this book are helpful in complying with the tax system as it exists right now. But if we all wake up and demand change from our politicians, we can make all those tips in this book obsolete.

We must call for a national commission to be put together, with representatives from across the country. This commission would include Members of Parliament from every political party. It would include tax accountants and tax lawyers, small-business owners, self-employed individuals from every industry and from every province, and average individual Canadian employees who file a tax return every year. The commission's mandate would be to undergo a comprehensive and complete review of the entire Canadian tax system from top to bottom, inside and out. It might take five years or even ten years but it is absolutely necessary.

We must put pressure on our politicians to come together, in a non-partisan fashion, on this issue. We might disagree about the ideal tax rate and the ideal amount of tax that people should pay. But we should all agree on the need to simplify the tax system.

My dream is for a simple tax system, as described in George's farewell letter. Let's make this happen. Contact your Member of Parliament, the Minister of Finance and the Prime Minister. You can find the contact information of your Member of Parliament by visiting the Government of Canada website: https://www.ourcommons.ca/en/contact-us.

ENDNOTES

The Making of a Grumpy Accountant

1   https://www.fraserinstitute.org/blogs/compliance-costs-and-complexity-in-canada-s-personal-income-tax

2   https://www.budget.gc.ca/2019/docs/plan/budget-2019-en.pdf Page 341 of the 2019 budget.

3   https://www.theglobeandmail.com/business/rob-magazine/article-when-even-the-pros-dont-understand-canadas-income-tax-system-you/

4   https://www.taxpolicycenter.org/briefing-book/what-other-countries-use-return-free-tax-filing

5   https://www.taxpolicycenter.org/briefing-book/what-other-countries-use-return-free-tax-filing

6   https://www.theatlantic.com/business/archive/2016/03/the-10-second-tax-return/475899/

7   https://www.cpacanada.ca/en/news/pivot-magazine/2019-05-07-tax-reform-bruce-ball

Chapter 1: Why is My Pay Cheque So Low?

8   Annual salary of $40,000 divided into 26 pay periods = gross pay of $1,538.46.

9   2020 tax rates assuming resident in Ontario – net pay would be $1,233.07.

Chapter 2: Are Tax Refunds a Huge Scam?

10   https://www.canada.ca/en/revenue-agency/corporate/about-canada-revenue-agency-cra/individual-income-tax-return-statistics.html

11   According to the Government of Canada's information from the 2016 year (https://www.canada.ca/en/department-finance/services/publications/federal-tax-expenditures/2019.html). I added up what the estimated amounts of all the tax credits and deductions cost the government in lost revenue. I excluded the principal residence exemption and partial inclusion of capital gains. The figure I calculated was $159 billion. According to the Fraser Institute, the figure is $130 billion (https://www.fraserinstitute.org/article/solve-canadas-tax-expenditure-problem-with-a-simpler-tax-system). To err on the safe side, I have used the lower figure of $130 billion.

12   Basic personal amount for the 2020 tax year. As at the time of this writing in 2020, the federal government has promised to increase this to $15,000 by 2023. All tax rates and amounts in the subsequent discussion are based on federal amounts only and exclude provincial amounts for the sake of easier readability.

13   https://www150.statcan.gc.ca/t1/tbl1/en/tv.action?pid=1110024101

14   The lowest federal tax bracket applies 15% federal tax to income up to $48,535.

15   https://www150.statcan.gc.ca/t1/tbl1/en/tv.action?pid=1110000801 – according to 2017 figures.

16   This is a rough estimate. I calculated this as per the numbers from Statistics Canada from the 2017 tax year (https://www150.statcan.gc.ca/t1/tbl1/en/tv.action?pid=1110000801).I took the number of tax filers in each tax bracket and calculated the amount of federal tax they would owe in each bracket and added it together. I used the high end of each tax bracket to err on the side of caution.

17   The 2020 tax bracket is from $48,536 to $97,069.

18   This is a rough estimate. I calculated this as per the numbers from Statistics Canada from the 2017 tax year (https://www150.statcan.gc.ca/t1/tbl1/en/tv.action?pid=1110000801). I took the number of tax filers in each tax bracket and calculated the amount of federal tax they would owe in each bracket and added it together. I used the high end of each tax bracket to err on the side of caution.

20   See Chapter 2, Are Tax Refunds a Huge Scam?

Chapter 3: No, You Cannot Deduct the Cost of Your Clothes!
[19] At the time of this writing in 2020.

Chapter 4: The Wonderful World of CRA Audits
[21] https://globalnews.ca/video/3880552/cra-freezes-mans-account-and-drains-payroll-after-promising-more-time-to-pay
[22] https://globalnews.ca/news/4626189/bradford-woman-canada-revenue-agency/
[23] https://www.advisor.ca/tax/tax-news/how-cra-spends-your-tax-dollars/
[24] https://www.advisor.ca/tax/tax-news/how-cra-spends-your-tax-dollars/
[25] https://www.advisor.ca/tax/tax-news/how-cra-spends-your-tax-dollars/
[26] https://nationalpost.com/news/canada-revenue-agency-still-giving-incorrect-information-on-tax-issues

Chapter 5: You Mean I Can Travel Back in Time?
[27] https://globalnews.ca/news/4681344/cra-issues-auditor-general/

Chapter 6: What's the Deal with GST Credits?
[28] GST Credit based on 2019 tax year amount per income of approximately $40,000 for a single individual.
[29] For the 2019 tax year; amount is approximate.
[30] Approximate combined federal + Ontario income tax in 2020.
[31] Assuming resident in Ontario.
[32] In the 2017-2018 fiscal year https://www.fin.gc.ca/afr-rfa/2018/report-rapport-eng.asp
[33] Based on 2019 combined federal and provincial tax rates and assuming resident in Ontario. For example, an individual who earns $21,500 of employment income will owe income tax of approximately $589 and receive $451 of GST Credits. So this person would be better off with zero income tax along with the elimination of GST Credits.
[34] The Canada Workers Benefit replaces and enhances the Working Income Tax Benefit, which is a tax credit that offsets tax on employment income for those with lower incomes, such that someone earning close to $20,000 a year in employment income will end up paying very little income tax. For example, an individual who earns $20,000 of employment income only owes $111.16 of income tax, assuming they are resident in Ontario, using 2019 tax rates.
[35] Amount at which Old Age Security (OAS) is clawed back in entirety for the 2020 year is $128,137. OAS begins to be clawed back at income of $79,054.
[36] These are estimates and an example of how a guaranteed minimum income would work in theory.
[37] https://www.pbo-dpb.gc.ca/en/blog/news/Guaranteed_Basic_Income
[38] Another similar system, favoured by conservative economists, such as Milton Friedman, would be a negative income tax.

Chapter 7: Take the Bonus
[39] Based on 2020 combined federal and provincial tax rates assuming resident in Ontario.
[40] Based on 2020 combined federal and provincial tax rates assuming resident in Ontario.
[41] Based on combined federal and Ontario tax rates for 2020.
[42] At the time of this writing in early 2020.

Chapter 9: Why Does the CRA Charge So Many Penalties?
[43] http://www.cbc.ca/news/business/canada-revenue-kpmg-secret-amnesty-1.3479594
[44] See Chapter 2, Are Tax Refunds a Huge Scam?
[46] See Chapter 6, What's the Deal with GST Credits?

Chapter 10: Love and Marriage

45   Assuming 2020 tax rates combined federal and Ontario.

Chapter 11: Home Sweet Home

47   Assume living in Ontario and paying provincial land transfer tax.

Chapter 12: Children – Little Bundles of Tax Benefits

48   At the time of this writing, a federal election had just concluded. During the campaign, both the Conservative and Liberal parties proposed making these benefits tax free, but the proposal has not been implemented by the new government. These benefits are still taxable as of the time of this writing.

49   Based on $150,000 of family net income for the 2018 tax year.

50   See Chapter 2, Are Tax Refunds a Huge Scam?

51   See Chapter 6, What's the Deal with GST Credits.

52   https://www.canada.ca/content/dam/cra-arc/prog-policy/stats/ccb-stats/2017-tax-year/ccb1-eng.pdf

53   As described in Chapter 2, Are Tax Refunds a Huge Scam?

54   Assume 2019 combined federal + Ontario tax rates.

55   As described in Chapter 10, Love and Marriage.

56   https://www.cpacanada.ca/en/the-cpa-profession/about-cpa-canada/key-activities/public-policy-government-relations/policy-advocacy/cpa-canada-tax-review-initiative/canadas-tax-system

57   https://www.cbc.ca/news/politics/cra-benefit-review-report-1.4841946

58   https://www.cbc.ca/news/politics/cra-benefit-review-report-1.4841946

Chapter 14: How to Save Money

59   At the time of this writing in 2020, mortgage interest rates are at historic lows.

Chapter 15: The Hardship of Being a Self-Employed Tax Collector

60   https://www150.statcan.gc.ca/n1/pub/71-222-x/71-222-x2019002-eng.htm

61   Some provinces have their own provincial sales tax authority, other provinces have the HST. The HST is the "Harmonized Sales Tax," which combines the federal GST and the provincial sales tax. For simplicity, I will only refer to GST since it applies across the country.

62   Rates in the year 2020, at time of writing.

Chapter 16: One Equals Two – Double CPP

63   Based on combined Federal + Ontario tax rates for 2020.

64   Based on 2020 CPP rates.

Chapter 17: Are Corporations Evil Legal Fictions?

65   https://nationalpost.com/pmn/news-pmn/canada-news-pmn/1-7m-award-for-b-c-couple-after-malicious-prosecution-by-canada-revenue-agency

66   Combined 2020 federal + Ontario corporate tax rate on "active business income" – that is, income eligible for the small business deduction on the first $500,000 of net income.

67   Combined federal + Ontario rate for 2020 on income above $220,001.

Chapter 19: Paying Tax on Imaginary Income

68   Another recent change, in 2018, for professionals, is something known as "work-in-progress." This is even more nefarious, complicated and unfair than what I just described above in regards to accounts receivable. Work-in-progress refers to work that has not yet

been completed or invoiced or billed to the customer yet must be included in income for the year! It's actually totally insane and completely nonsensical. A small-business owner professional, such as a lawyer or accountant, must calculate, at their year-end date, how much income is in progress. This refers to client work that is not yet complete but has begun. So the work is not completed but the government expects one to actually calculate and place a value on the work using very complex calculations and then adding that to one's taxable income for the year! This is, in my opinion, absolutely pure insanity. Only someone who never ran a small business in their life can come up with such nonsense. Has anyone in the current Federal government (in 2018 under Prime Minister Justin Trudeau and Finance Minister Bill Morneau) ever run their own small business? Do they actually believe it's logical that a small-business owner should have to increase their income, therefore increasing their taxes payable, on the basis of work that's not complete or even near completion? How does that make any sense at all? It's just so unfair, punitive and frustrating. I would obviously propose to abolish this new aspect of taxation for professionals and service providers and simply, as described above, let all small-business owners use the cash basis of accounting for tax purposes to keep things simple, fair and realistic in terms of cash flow for small-business owners.

Chapter 20: The Golden Years

[69] Maximum amount for 2020 assuming one starts to receive CPP at 65 years of age.

[70] Maximum amount for 2020 for an individual assuming they start to receive OAS at 65 years of age.

[71] 2020 figure.

[72] 2020 figure.

[73] https://www150.statcan.gc.ca/n1/pub/11-630-x/11-630-x2016002-eng.htm

[74] https://www12.statcan.gc.ca/census-recensement/2016/as-sa/98-200-x/2016013/98-200-x2016013-eng.cfm

[75] https://www.budget.gc.ca/2019/docs/plan/budget-2019-en.pdf Page 291 of the federal budget for the 2017-2018 fiscal year.

Chapter 21: Death and Taxes – There is No Escape

[76] https://globalnews.ca/video/3338347/new-brunswick-man-receives-unexpectedly-morbid-letter-from-cra

[77] https://globalnews.ca/news/4293120/canada-revenue-agency-dead-people-errors/

Chapter 22: My Dream for the Future

[78] https://www.theglobeandmail.com/business/rob-magazine/article-when-even-the-pros-dont-understand-canadas-income-tax-system-you/

[79] Total federal government debt and provincial debt across all provinces as of this writing in early 2020.

[80] https://globalnews.ca/video/3194348/canada-revenue-agency-will-monitor-your-facebook

RESOURCES

Some of these links and resources may be out of date at the time you are reading this. Visit www.grumpyaccountant.ca for the continuously updated list of resources.

Bookkeeping and Expense Tracking Tools

Quickbooks:
>https://quickbooks.intuit.com/ca/

Veryfi:
>www.veryfi.com

Wave:
>www.waveapps.com

Mileage tracking:
>www.driversnote.ca

CRA Online Links

Canada Child Benefits, Apply for:
>https://www.canada.ca/en/revenue-agency/services/child-family-benefits/canada-child-benefit-overview/canada-child-benefit-apply.html

Canada Pension Plan, Rates and Information:
>https://www.canada.ca/en/revenue-agency/services/tax/businesses/topics/payroll/payroll-deductions-contributions/canada-pension-plan-cpp/cpp-contribution-rates-maximums-exemptions.html

Disability Tax Credit:
>https://www.canada.ca/en/revenue-agency/services/tax/individuals/segments/tax-credits-deductions-persons-disabilities/disability-tax-credit.html

EI Benefits, Apply for:
https://www.canada.ca/en/services/benefits/ei/ei-regular-benefit/apply.html

EI Rates and Information:
https://www.canada.ca/en/revenue-agency/services/tax/businesses/topics/payroll/payroll-deductions-contributions/employment-insurance-ei/ei-premium-rates-maximums.html

Form RC4288—Request for Taxpayer Relief to Waive Penalties and Interest:
https://www.canada.ca/en/revenue-agency/services/forms-publications/forms/rc4288.html

Form T1213 to Request to Reduce Tax Deductions:
https://www.canada.ca/en/revenue-agency/services/forms-publications/forms/t1213.html

Form T2125 Statement of Business or Professional Activities:
https://www.canada.ca/en/revenue-agency/services/forms-publications/forms/t2125.html

Form T2200 Declaration of Conditions of Employment (Employment Expenses):
https://www.canada.ca/en/revenue-agency/services/forms-publications/forms/t2200.html

Form T776 Statement of Real Estate Rentals:
https://www.canada.ca/en/revenue-agency/services/forms-publications/forms/t776.html

Form T777 Employment Expenses:
https://www.canada.ca/en/revenue-agency/services/forms-publications/forms/t777.html

Fraud, Information on and Reporting:
https://www.canada.ca/en/revenue-agency/corporate/security/protect-yourself-against-fraud.html

GST/HST Guide:
https://www.canada.ca/en/revenue-agency/services/forms-publications/publications/rc4022.html

GST/HST, Quick Method:

https://www.canada.ca/en/revenue-agency/services/forms-
publications/publications/rc4058/quick-method-accounting-gst-
hst.html

"My Account" for Individuals, Set Up:

https://www.canada.ca/en/revenue-agency/services/e-services/e-
services-individuals/account-individuals.html

"My Business Account," Set Up:

https://www.canada.ca/en/revenue-agency/services/e-services/
e-services-businesses/business-account.html

"My Service Canada Account," Set Up:

https://www.canada.ca/en/employment-social-development/
services/my-account.html

Payroll Source Deductions Calculator:

https://www.canada.ca/en/revenue-agency/services/e-services/
e-services-businesses/payroll-deductions-online-calculator.html

Tax Services Office and Tax Centre, Find Your:

https://www.canada.ca/en/revenue-agency/corporate/contact-
information/tax-services-offices-tax-centres.html

Do-It-Yourself Tax Filing Software

Use CRA auto-fill system in conjunction with these.

Simple Tax:

www.simpletax.ca

TurboTax:

turbotax.intuit.ca

UFile:

www.ufile.ca

Studio Tax:

www.studiotax.com

Investment Advice and General Personal Finance

Book Recommendations:

The Wealthy Barber by David Chilton

The Wealthy Barber Returns by David Chilton

Canadian in a T-shirt:
https://facebook.com/CanadianTShirt (search for his YouTube channel)

Couch Potato Investing:
https://canadiancouchpotato.com/

www.cutthecrapinvesting.com

www.howtosavemoney.ca

www.moneysense.ca

www.practicalmoneyskills.ca

Other Resources and Information

Canada Pension Plan:
www.cppib.com

GST/HST by Province:
https://canadabusiness.ca/government/taxes-gst-hst/federal-tax-information/overview-of-charging-and-collecting-sales-tax/

Tax Tips:
www.taxtips.ca

Phone Numbers

CRA business enquiries line: 1-800-959-5525

CRA individual enquiries line: 1-800-959-8281

Report Fraud: 1-888-495-8501

Service Canada: 1-800-622-6232

Retirement Planning

Apply for CPP:
https://www.canada.ca/en/services/benefits/publicpensions/cpp/
cpp-benefit/apply.html

Apply for OAS:
https://www.canada.ca/en/services/benefits/publicpensions/cpp/
old-age-security/apply.html

Retirement Income Calculator:
https://www.canada.ca/en/services/benefits/publicpensions/cpp/
retirement-income-calculator.html

www.retirehappy.ca

Tax Calculators

https://neuvoo.ca/tax-calculator/

https://www.ey.com/ca/en/services/tax/tax-calculators

https://www.eytaxcalculators.com/en/2020-personal-tax-calculator.html

ACKNOWLEDGEMENTS

First, I am thankful to all Canadians for complacently allowing our government to create such a complicated tax system. Without that happening, I would never have the opportunity to write *The Grumpy Accountant*. Likewise, I am grateful and would like to acknowledge the past 50 years of politicians who have been in power and did, quite literally, nothing to simplify our tax system. Without you, I would not be able to earn a living and would not have written this book.

When I became very serious about writing *The Grumpy Accountant*, I e-mailed the author of *The Wealthy Barber* and *The Wealthy Barber Returns*, David Chilton, to seek his permission and blessing for writing my book in a similar format to his. He called me back within ten minutes and encouraged me to move forward with the project. He gave me invaluable advice that forced me to really focus and re-think the purpose of the book. His online book marketing course, The Chilton Method (www.thechilton method.com), which he advised me to take, was extremely helpful.

Heidy Lawrance and her team at wemakebooks.ca have made the option of self-publishing a practical reality. She was extremely patient with me and her advice and expertise have been crucial to this project. Catherine Leek, the editor, did an amazing job. Her patience, honesty and helpful feedback was critical in turning my writing into something coherent and readable.

Peter Bowerman is the author of *The Well-Fed Self-Publisher* (wellfedsp.com). He offers his advice and expertise to self-publishers and helped tremendously with a few specific aspects of this book.

My fellow accountant colleagues, Allan Gutenberg and George Farkas, read through the entire book and provided very valuable and thoughtful feedback. My friends, Jonathan Farkas and Valerie Haboucha, along with my loyal client, Iram Blajchman, my dear father Paul Winokur and my beloved wife Alison also read through the entire book and provided very important, brutally honest feedback and advice that I am extremely thankful for.

My dad is one of the wisest people that I know. As an actuary, he is extremely knowledgeable and insightful and provided very helpful advice regarding every aspect of the book.

I'd like to thank my mother, Sherry, for teaching me how to read when I was a young child and for always encouraging me to read books when I was growing up. More recently, I am very thankful that she called me a "grumpy old man" at a family dinner, after I spent an hour complaining about everything I felt was wrong with society. The word "grumpy" stuck in my head and I knew I could eventually put it to a good productive use.

Lastly, I must thank my incredible wife Alison for putting up with me. While I was spending countless hours writing this book, she has been taking care of our baby. She gave me the original idea to write down my thoughts. Every day, after work, I would complain to her about how inefficient our tax system is. She grew tired of my complaints but suggested I write a blog or some articles and that was the start of collecting my thoughts into what eventually became *The Grumpy Accountant*. Without her support, this project would not have been possible.

INDEX

Accrual accounting, 160-161, 164

Amortization, 157

Arbitrary assessment, 59-64

Audits, 27-37
    cost to taxpayers, 31
    GST, 119-120
    malicious auditors, 137-138
    Notice of Reassessment, 27
    payroll, 149-150

Bonus/Increase in income, 53-56
    do the math, 54
    exceptions to taking bonus, 54-55
    impact on tax bracket, 53-54
    RRSP to eliminate tax on, 54

Canada Child Benefit. *See* Children.

Canada Pension Plan. *See* CCP.

Canada Revenue Agency. *See* CRA.

Capital assets, 156-163

Carter Commission Report, The, 33

Cash-basis accounting, 161

Children, 89-96
    Canada Child Benefit, 90
    child care deduction, 97
    hiring a nanny, 97-101
    maternity benefits, 89-90
    RESP, 103-104
    staying home, 91-92

CPP. *See also* Retirement planning.
    and retirement, 166
    death benefit, 181
    definition, 4
    impact of increase in income, 55
    when incorporated, 148
    when self-employed, 131-132

CRA
    audit. *See* Audits.
    Authorization Representative form, 60
    collections department, 28, 61-63
    double dipping on interest, 69
    freeze bank accounts, 30, 61-62
    garnish salaries, 30, 61-62
    mistakenly declare taxpayer dead,
      179-180
    My Account, 18, 65
    My Business Account, 133, 135
    payroll accounts, opening, 151
    Represent a Client system, 28
    taxpayer relief department, 68

Death of a taxpayer, 180-185.
    See also Last surviving spouse.
    CPP death benefit, 181
    final tax return, 181-182
    life insurance proceeds, 181
    mistaken declaration by CRA, 179-180
    notifying Service Canada, et al, 181

Deductions
    charitable donations, 10
    child care, 97
    medical, 10
    small business, 123
    student loan interest, 10

Depreciation, 157

EI
  definition, 4
  increase in income, impact on, 55
  maternity benefits, 89-90

Employer, becoming, 97-101
  audit, 99-100
  CPP, EI and income tax, 97-98
  legal pay stub, 98
  nil remittance, 98-99
  payroll account, 97

Employment Insurance. See EI.

Expenses
  business, 23-24
  employee claims, 23
  self-employed, 129
  versus capital assets, 156-163

George's dream, 187-194
  take action, 195

George's pet peeves
  administrative bureaucracy/costs,
    33, 46, 62, 93
  automated CRA notices, 63
  complaints and appeals, 71, 100, 141
  CRA's lack of timeliness, 32, 41-42
  lack of internal communication, 46,
    123-124, 141, 150
  lack of transparency, 72,
  outdated RRSP system, 168-169
  patriarchal approach, 14, 47, 84-85
  self-employed and GST, 116-125
  small business assets and depreciation,
    157-158
  tax refunds, 11-12
  total vs. combined family income,
    76-77

George's solutions
  cash-basis accounting for small
    businesses, 161
  CRA to verify receipts first, 32

eliminate deductions and credits,
    14-16, 31, 42, 93-94, 173
  eliminate filing returns for employees,
    71-72
  eliminate income tax on first $50,000,
    48, 79, 173
  file as a family unit, 79
  flat-rate penalty for late filing, 72
  for GST and self-employed, 124-125
  for retirement planning, 171-175
  GST Credits annually only, 46
  guaranteed minimum income, 49, 50
    79, 93-94
  increase small supplier GST limit, 122
  no penalties for missed T slips, 72
  power to waive penalties for CRA
    agents, 72
  pre-filled tax returns, 72
  re-direct transfers, 49-50
  reduce administrative bureaucracy, 47
  self-employed income reporting, 130
  three categories of income, 50

GIS, 167. See also Retirement planning.

Goods and Services. See GST and
  GST Credits.

Government programs
  benefits end upon death, 179
  Canada Child Benefits, 49, 90
  Canada Education Savings Grant, 104
  Canada Workers Benefit, 49
  Disability Tax Credit, 170
  first-time Home Buyers' Tax Credit, 84
  GIS, 49
  GST credit, 45-52
  Home Buyers' Plan, 83
  OAS, 49
  tuition credit, 40

Gross pay, 2

GST
  installments, 133

quick method for calculating, 122-123
self-employed, 116-125

GST Credits
abuse of system, 47-48
definition, 45
impact of increase in income, 55
when married, 76

Guaranteed Income Supplement.
See GIS and Retirement planning.

Guaranteed Minimum Income, 49, 93
cost, 50
who's eligible, 50

Home ownership, 83-87
declaring sale of home, 84
Home Buyer's Plan, 83
land transfer tax rebate, 84
renting a portion. *See* Renting part
of your home.
using RRSP, 110

Income tax return
failing to file, 59-61

Income War Measures Act, 6

Incorporating a business, 137-144
corporate tax rate, 139-140
goodwill asset, 143
paying yourself, 148-152
payroll audit, 149-150
provincial vs. federal, 140
sell assets, 142-144
separate tax return (T2), 138-139
tax deferral, 139-140

Industry Canada, 141-142

Investing, 113

Last surviving spouse, 183-185
capital gains, 183

deemed disposition, 183-184
estate income continues to earn, 184

Marriage, 75-81
file separately, 75
credits and deductions, 75-77
investment income, 78-79
minimizing tax, 77

Net income, 22-23

Notice of Assessment, 17

Notice of Collection, 61

Notice of Reassessment, 27

OAS, 166. *See also* Retirement planning.
and retirement, 167
clawback, 167-168

Old Age Security. *See* OAS.

Penalties, 67-73
failing to file return, 60-61
GST installments, late, 117
GST returns, late, 117
overcontributions, 112
wealthiest avoid, 67-68

Pre-Assessment Review, 29-30

Registered Education Savings Plans.
See RESP.

Registered Retirement Income Fund.
See RRIF.

Registered Retirement Savings Plan.
See RRSP.

Renting part of your home, 85-86
income not tax free, 85
principal residence status, 85

Resources, 201-205

RESP, 103-104
  Canada Education Savings Grant, 104
  maximum contributions, 104
  withdrawal, 103

Retirement planning, 165-175
  age of retirement, 167-169
  CPP, 166
  Disability Tax Credit, 170
  GIS, 167
  income splitting, 170
  minimize tax vs. maximize benefits,
    170-171
  OAS, 167
  RRSP vs. RRIF, 168
  TFSA, 169-170

RRIF, 168-169.
  See also Retirement planning.
  holding annuities, 168
  versus RRSP in retirement, 168

RRSP, 103, 105-106, 166.
  See also Retirement planning.
  age 71, 106, 168
  disadvantages, 106
  Home Buyer's Plan, 83, 110
  overcontributions, 112
  tax refunds, 105
  versus pay debt, 106
  versus RRIF in retirement, 168
  versus TFSA, 107
  withdrawals, 105

Saving money, 103-113
  investments, 113
  RESP, 103-104
  RRSP, 105-106
  TFSA, 106-109

Self-employment, 115-125
  cash flow, 117-118
  CPP, 131-132
  goodwill asset, 143
  GST, 116-121
  GST issues, solutions, 122-125
  incorporating.
    See Incorporating a business.
  multi-tasking, 123
  My Business Account, 133
  penalties, 117
  tracking expenses, 129

T4 slip, 4, 6, 9, 70-71
  arbitrary assessment, 59-64
  tax return, 16

T4A slip, 70-71

Tax brackets
  explained, 15-16
  impact on bonus/raise, 53-56

Tax deferral, 139-140

Tax Free Savings Accounts. See TFSA.

Tax refund, 10
  reduce deductions at source, 13
  tax-free loan to government, 11-13

Tax return
  adjustments, past returns, 40
  filing, 4-5
  failing to file, 59-61

TFSA, 103, 106-109
  and retirement, 169-170
  contributions, 107
  overcontributions, 112
  versus RRSP, 107, 170

Tips
    accessing credits, 52
    adjusting past returns, 43
    apply for all credits and benefits, 96
    avoid penalties and interest, 74
    communicate with spouse, 81
    CRA letters, don't stress, 65
    develop bookkeeping skills, 128
    employees' business expenses, 25
    estate planning, 186
    extra income, questioning, 57
    file returns on time, 64, 74
    get help, 101
    GST, set-up from start, 126-127
    home ownership, implications of, 87
    incorporate vs. not incorporating, 145
    keep up to date, 101
    keeping receipts, 35, 101
    maximize RRSP, RESP, TFSA, 110-111
    methods to file tax returns, 20
    My Account, 18
    never assume in small business, 164
    overcontributions to RRSP or TFSA, 112
    pay stubs, 7
    paying yourself from corporation, 153-154
    reducing tax deductions at source, 19
    retirement planning, 176-177
    scams, 36-37
    take action, 195
    tax installments, save for, 134-135
    watch fees on investments, 113

US citizens, 107, 112

Voluntary Disclosure Program, 69-70